The Urban Vineyard

A guide to growing grapes in your garden or on an allotment and making your own great tasting wine

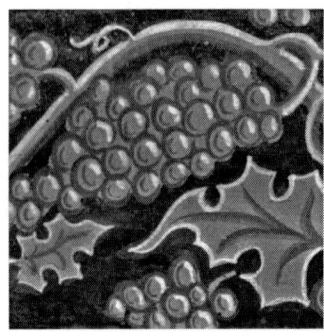

"With interest in city gardens and rooftop farming booming around the world, Paul Olding's *The Urban Vineyard* adds a fresh and intoxicating voice to the conversation. Amateur vintners will find this both a comprehensive guide to the art and science of urban winemaking, and a compelling narrative of one man's quest to make great wine in the middle of a bustling metropolis"
Steven Johnson, author Where Good Ideas Come From

"Paul is a great television director, but it turns out he's also a great writer, vintner, vigneron and above all, dreamer. This book is a guide to making your own wine in the city, but it's also a book that encourages the reader to follow their passions, ambitions and dreams and make things happen in the most unlikely of places. I love that."
Prof Brian Cox, physicist and author Why Does e=mc²

"Bursting with bright advice with top notes of joyful family enterprise and packed with persuasive reasons to give it a go, this is a book that needs no laying down. Enjoy immediately."
Richard Reynolds, author On Guerrilla Gardening

"This book is a good read and will also help the newcomer to our rapidly growing industry take their interest into reality. Enjoy reading and perhaps taking your dreams into reality with wine from your own vines."
Paul Langham, Chairman United Kingdom Vineyards Association

The Urban Vineyard

A guide to growing grapes in your
garden or on an allotment and
making your own great tasting wine

Paul Olding

Foreword by Richard Reynolds
author, *On Guerilla Gardening*

Published by the Author
April 2015

Copyright © 2015 by Paul Olding

Email: paul@paulolding.co.uk

The right of Paul Olding to be identified as the author of this work has been asserted by him in accordance with the Copyright, Designs and Patents Act of 1988

First Published in paperback in Great Britain in 2015

Photographs & Illustrations Copyright © 2015 Paul Olding

All rights reserved. No part of this publication may be reproduced, stored in a retrieval system, or transmitted, in any form or by any means, electrical, mechanical, photocopying, recording or otherwise, without the prior written permission of the publisher.

The information provided in this book is true and complete to the best of the knowledge of the author. All recommendations are made without guarantee on the part of the author. The author disclaims any liability in connection with the use of this information.

A CIP catalogue record for this book is available from the British Library

ISBN: 978-1-326-09224-5

What did the grape say when he got stepped on?
Nothing, but he let out a little wine.

Christmas Cracker, 2011

Contents

Acknowledgements	xii
Foreword by Richard Reynolds	xiii
Preface	xv
1. So It Begins	**1**
English (and Welsh) Wine	2
Terroir	5
Growing Grapes in Great Britain	6
2. Urban Spaces	**11**
Gardens & Community Spaces	11
Allotments	12
3. Preparing the Ground	**17**
Altitude	17
Frost, Wind and Sunshine	18
Preparing the Soil	20
Grass & Weed Removal	22
Compost Bins	23
Assessing Soil Structure	25
Improving Soil Texture	27
Installing a DIY Drainage System	30
Materials & Design	31
Venting the Water	34
4. Choosing Your Vines	**35**
Grape Varietals	37
Interspecific Hybrids	39
Rootstock	41
Soil Analysis	42

vii

5. Urban Vineyard Design — 45
- Grapevines in the Garden — 45
- Vineyard Design for an Allotment — 47
- Vineyard Orientation — 48
- Vine Spacing & Soil Fertility — 49
- Distance Between the Rows — 51

6. Between the Rows — 55
- Grass Alleys — 55
- Vegetables in the Vineyard? — 56
- Raised Beds — 57

7. Planting Your Urban Vineyard — 61
- Preparing the Plants — 61
- Preparing the Ground (Again) — 62
- Planting your Vines — 66

8. The First Years — 71
- Weeds — 71
- Watering — 73
- Vine Growth — 74
- End of Year 1 — 76
- Year 2 — 77

9. Installing a Trellis — 79
- Vertical Shoot Position (VSP) Trellis — 82
- Installing a VSP Trellis in the Garden — 82
- Fruiting & Foliage Wires — 84
- Installing a VSP Trellis on Open Ground — 85
- End Posts — 86
- Anchoring the End Posts — 88
- In-Line Posts — 89
- Wire & Tensioning — 90
- Installing the Support Wire & Fruiting Wire — 91
- Foliage Wires — 94

10. Vegetables in the Vineyard — 97
- Constructing Raised Beds — 98
- Potatoes — 101
- Squashes — 102
- Beans — 104
- Strawberries — 106
- Raspberries — 106
- Corn — 108
- Other Vegetables — 108
- Leeks — 109
- Green Manure — 110
- Onions and Garlic — 111
- Bug Hotel — 112
- Complimentary Planting — 114
- Watering — 114

11. Year by Year Canopy Management & Annual Winter Pruning — 119
- Year 1 — 119
- Year 2 — 120
- Beginning of Year 3 — 122
- During Year 3 — 123
- Year 4 — 125
- Cane & Spur vs Cordon & Spur — 126
- The *Guyot* System — 128
- Annual Winter Pruning for *Guyot* — 129
- Next Year's Fruiting Canes — 132
- Next Year's Spurs — 134
- Cordon & Spur Management — 136
- Year 5 and Onwards — 136
- Cuttings — 137

12. Additional Canopy Management Activities — 139
- Bud Rubbing — 140
- Flowering — 141
- Tucking In — 142
- Topping Off — 143
- Disease Control — 144

Nutritional Deficiencies	145
Animal Pests	147

13. The Grape Harvest — 149

Balance	150
The First Harvest	151
Cluster Thinning	152
Leaf Pulling	152
Netting your Crop	154
The Path to Harvest	157
Sugar Levels	158
Refractometer	160
Sugar vs Acid	162
Harvest Day	165

14. The Kitchen Winery — 169

Inventory	170
Preparing the Must	171
Sterilisation	171
Destemming	172
Crushing	174
Must Preservation	177

15. Making White & Rosé Still Wine — 179

Resting on the Skins	180
The Grape Press	181
Pressing	184
Demijohns	188
Settling & Racking Off	189
Acid Levels	191
Chaptalisation	193
Bentonite	196
Fermentation	197
Slowing the Ferment	200
Oak	202

16. Making Red Wine	**203**
Adjustments	204
The Ferment	204
Pushing Down	205
Pressing	206
Post Pressing Fermentation	207
Maderisation	207
Hydrogen Sulphide	208
Record Keeping	210
17. The Bottled Vintage	**211**
Dry vs Medium	212
End of the Ferment	213
Fining	215
Cold Stabilisation	216
Bottling	217
Sweetening	220
Blending	221
Corking	222
Finishing Touches	224
How Many Bottles?	226
Cellar	226
When to Drink?	227
Epilogue	**229**
Additional Reading	**231**
Online Resources	**233**
Index	**235**

Acknowledgements

I would like to thank the *Guerilla Gardener* Richard Reynolds for giving invaluable feedback on the book, and for writing the foreword. I would also like to thank all my family for making my Urban Vineyard possible in the first place - my wife Andrea, my two sons Huw and Evan, my in-laws Vic and Carol and my mother Enid. As you will find out, when I was initially setting up the site, it was all hands on deck. Then throughout the years, everyone has had a hand in picking the grapes, making the wine and sharing in a bottle or two. My father-in-law Vic has been a continual source of horticultural knowledge and physical manpower on the vineyard. I would also like to thank my dad Frank who sowed the seed of interest back when I was a child, with his own attempts at making home brew in our kitchen. I think he would have enjoyed my wine. *Salut!*

Foreword

"You what?" That's the double take you will get when telling someone you make your own wine from your own grapes here in Britain. "Are you bonkers?" As a guerrilla gardener I too am used to raising eyebrows because I defy several conventions by snatching scraps of shabby public land and make them productive without permission. This book is giving gardening another much needed twist and I encourage you to delight in challenging perceptions. You're holding a radical manifesto! Growing and eating pak choi was until a few years ago saddled by similar scepticism driven by geography and cautious taste buds, but now they only register a flutter of surprise in the most traditional corners of our gardening nation. Even growing tomatoes to eat was seriously frowned upon until the 19th century and now they're one of the most popular grow-your-owns.

I joined Paul's epic journey towards becoming an expert urban vigneron a few years ago at the most important part in the whole process, the annual tasting party held in his kitchen winery. We would be about to find out, was his effort really worth it? And can you be sure from putting Paul's words into action that you'll be glugging something to be proud of? Well yes it was and yes I think you can. I discovered that afternoon Paul had crafted splendid wines. I came to Paul's party positively inclined to enjoy myself because I'm a fairly regular drinker of English wines. I'd initially dabbled out of curiosity, patriotism and my love of the underdog. Since my experimental tasting, I've bought English wines by the box-load. At the party, few of Paul's other guests were enthusiastic English wine drinkers but despite that, there was still plenty of genuine and positive surprise in the room (and absolutely no spitting). These were thirsty converts. So follow our author's advice and you'll be OK.

It helps when wine making from scratch if you can soak up some of Paul's personality. He is part romantic, part scientist and has enough bloody-minded determination to succeed against the odds, be it boggy ground, birds, bad weather, botrytis or Boots The Chemist. That last challenge required Paul to convince the pharmacist he required bigger kicks than booze to get his highs if he was to secure a crucial piece of equipment necessary for wine making. That awkward moment is one he's been through so you hopefully don't have to. And, as you'll see, a wonderful family helps too. This book is filled throughout with Paul's supporting cast and crew of relatives. He has surely started a new wine making dynasty, to become the *Gallos* of southeast London. Paul's ever-present sage, his father-in-law, looms large as the allotmenteer for life, who regularly solves a conundrum. Think of this book as for you what Paul's father-in-law is to him, and then some.

There's no doubt an urban vigneron requires persistence, patience and persuasion. If you're at the radish stage of grow-your-own gardening then recognize now that drink-your-own gardening requires not just a few weeks between sowing and consuming but a few years. Good things come to those that wait, and it's even more so for your own wine as it is for *Guinness*.

I'm inspired. So far I have hops growing on a traffic island near Lambeth North but it's early days making this crop work and I haven't had a successful harvest. Meanwhile I have mastered the simple act of growing and harvesting lavender from which we make fragrant pillows and occasionally biscuits. There are guerrilla gardeners closer to achieving grape to glass completeness. I've discovered one who has planted vines in parks and I've heard from several guerrilla grape pickers - one propagated a vine from the seed of a grape she plucked from an Australian winery. With Paul's guide to hand we can enjoy our own wine from new terroir, whether it is your back garden or back street.

Richard Reynolds, author *On Guerrilla Gardening*

Preface

This book is for people who like to dream. It's both a *How To* guide and a personal account of how I brought one of my own dreams to life - to have my own urban vineyard. As you'll soon discover, I grow grapevines both in my back garden at home and on a small allotment in southeast London, then convert the annual grape harvest into delicious homemade wine in a temporary winery I set up in my kitchen. I'm not an expert Vigneron or Vintner by any stretch of the imagination, and I don't come from a long family lineage of wine makers, but now in the eighth year of practical experience managing my urban vineyard, plus an additional five years prior to that reading, studying and visiting commercial vineyards (and dabbling in shop-bought home brew wine kits), I feel I have enough knowledge to help any would-be urban wine making enthusiast to grow grapes and make some great tasting urban wine.

I'm one of those people that like to write *To Do* lists, and not just one list, but various categories of list. These lists grow, things get struck off on completion, there are priority lists that need to be attended to TODAY (not sure capital letters make it any more urgent). Whilst I do get things done, to my knowledge I've never totally completed everything on any one of my many lists - any leftovers get added to the next list and so on. Quite a while back, a list emerged simply entitled 'Books'. This wasn't books I thought I should *read*, but books I hoped I might *write*. Along with potential titles on photography and assorted travelogues (both great passions of mine), plus perhaps a treatise on how to be a television Producer (for that is my current day job), I had the idea of writing about my urban vineyard and how it came to be.

I'm a scientist by training (a biologist with a doctorate in small, noisy Australian tree frogs) and a planner at heart, and I like to have a rigorously tested plan before I start anything. This can get a little wearing (and possibly quite annoying to my family and work colleagues), as I want to be confident I can see a start, middle and end to an idea before I embark on it. So too with the notion of writing a book about my vineyard (and indeed, with setting up the vineyard itself). The first hurdle was to work out the range and scope of my book and what I might call it.

At first I had 'The Allotment Vintner' as the title. It sounded pretty catchy, but a *Vintner* is someone who just makes wine. I say *just* in no sense to belittle the glorious and multifaceted art of the master

wine maker who employ techniques passed down through the generations to turn grape juice into wine. But my book was to be much more than *just* about making wine.

I intended for the book to have lots of self help information about how to grow the grapes I use to make my wine, so I thought it's title should reflect this. I decided on 'The Allotment Vigneron', after the French word for grape grower. But I felt again this title narrowed the scale and ambition of the book. I wanted my book to be more inclusive and cover the growing of grapevines anywhere in the urban environment, whether that be a couple of vines in your back garden, in a pot on a patio, down on an allotment or indeed on some other urban plot, perhaps as part of a community project. In this vein it even dials into the growing movement of Guerrilla Gardening whose activists bring life to ignored land, curb sides and roundabouts in our concrete jungles (*Guerrilla Viticulture* perhaps?). So now I was in a right pickle. If the book had 'allotment' in the title, it may not appeal to those *without* an allotment. If I called it 'Allotment and Garden' it would certainly expand the potential interest base, but it was now getting a bit wordy. Maybe I should spell out the scope of the book in a subtitle?

I got thinking about what makes this book different, it's so-called *Unique Selling Point* or USP. It's certainly not a guide to establishing and running a vast commercial vineyard, many of which are springing up all over southern England and Wales (and even up to Yorkshire). No, this book is about sharing my experiences of growing grapevines slap bang in the middle of the (sub)urban jungle and how you too could grow grapes to make gorgeous wine anywhere in the urban habitat. So I came to the title 'The Urban Vineyard'.

This book tells the story of how I created my urban vineyard and how each year I harvest the fruits of my labour and make my own delicious homemade wine. It also provides a step by step guide for all would-be urban Vignerons and Vintners (not just in Britain, but anywhere in the world), to show how it's an entirely reasonable prospect to grow grapevines in an urban environment and to transform your home grown grapes into one of the most noble and loveliest drinks known to Humanity.

1. So It Begins

For many years I wanted a vineyard. It was a dream of mine to plant and nurture my own grapevines, to make and drink my own wine. It all started on honeymoon in Australia. Prior to this, I was never really a fan of wine. At school, alcoholic beverages never interested me, not by some moral choice, but as far as I recall, because I just didn't like the taste of the assorted drinks my school friends managed to consume in vast quantities. But at university, the social side of college rowing introduced me to the delights of *Pimms* and from *Pimms* came an assortment of sweet alcoholic beverages. The invention of the alcopop was right up my street, but wine was still never on the agenda.

So to the turn of the millennium and the honeymoon in Australia. I was sat with the new Mrs Olding on the balcony of the restaurant at a campsite in Nitmiluk National Park (aka Katherine Gorge) after a fabulous day walking in the bush and swimming in the water. With the sun setting behind the distant gum trees, for some reason, a glass of wine just seemed the right thing to have. So we ordered a bottle and it was good. So began my love affair with wine.

Since that turning point in the Australian outback well over a decade ago, I've grown not just to love drinking wine, but to love

growing grapevines and to enjoy employing the ages-old techniques to ferment the juice of its berries. But this has been more a *ménage à trois* as opposed to a straight forward love affair, as there are two loves that have blossomed - wine and English wine.

English (and Welsh) Wine

English Wine, for many, still comes as the punchline of a joke or a comedy anecdote passed down from someone who once tasted it some decades ago. For many people, their opinion of English Wine stems from a taste of something their dad may have made at home during the 1970s, possibly not using grapes, but assorted fruits, often picked at the side of the road (creating  something called *Country Wine*). I remember bubbling demijohns sitting on top of the freezer in our brown kitchen circa 1978, where my father (like so many other dads at the time) had purchased all the kit from Boots the Chemist (you'll struggle to find any wine making stuff there now). But English wine is so much more than the hobbyist dabblings of 1970s dads.

While still very much in its infancy compared to the rest of the wine-growing world, wine made commercially in England (and Wales)  is now a significant and continually expanding, multi-award winning enterprise. Admittedly, the scale of production is still quite small - if you try to find *English Wine* in a world wine almanac, you may be lucky with a single mention if you look hard enough. Yet I truly believe that English wine is a blossoming addition to the New World of wine and should be ignored at your peril.

So It Begins

White Castle Vineyard, Monmouthshire, Wales

Growing grapevines in England and Wales is nothing new, with the first vines brought over by the Romans. These vines were actually smuggled into Britannia illegally as emperor *Domitan* (AD81 - 96) had banned the growing of vines outside of Italy. Then, with the onset of the Dark Ages, while we lost (or somehow forgot) many of the Roman customs and assorted technologies, growing grapevines and making wine persisted. The Saxons still dabbled, with records made of the *Wyn Moneth* or month of the wine harvest which took place in October. Vineyards in England have been noted in assorted historical documents throughout the last 2000 years, including the famous Doomsday book of 1088 recording some 30 - 40 vineyards (the Normans kept the vineyards going to supply their monasteries with communion wine). But around the time Henry II married Eleanor of Aquitaine (1152), there appears to have been a distinct drop in wine production. Eleanor was blessed with the dowry of the *Garonne* district of France and all its wine growing lands, and so most of England's wine was imported from France - something that continues to this day, with wine imports from across Europe and the rest of the world only really kicking in within the last few decades.

The subsequent dissolution of the monasteries in the 1500s by Henry VIII, plus what some believe to be the onset of a cold period called the 'Little Ice Age' helped kill off many of England's remaining vineyards. But some hung on. English vineyards pop up in assorted writings from the 1700s, but it wasn't until the twentieth century that oenologically minded pioneers took up the mantle once again. While a few people started to investigate the notion of growing grapes in the 1930s, the modern resurgence in Britain did not really begin until post WW2, with Sir Guy Salisbury-Jones setting up the first modern commercial vineyard at Hambledon in 1952. In 1973, he even exported some of his English wine to France and Germany.

Denbies Wine Estate, Dorking, Surrey

Within the last 20 years or so, English wine has undergone a renaissance, not just in the number of people making it and the

So It Begins

number of bottles produced, but in its quality, with bottles finding their way out of the vineyard tasting rooms (or *Cellar Doors*) into farmers markets, high class restaurants, the cellars of swanky department stores, onto the shelves of supermarkets and shipped abroad. Then there are the international wine awards English wine has started to win, including the likes of Decanter magazine, where English fizz has beaten French Champagne. In the last decade or so, it's actually sparkling wine which has become the newest wave of the new wave of English wine, with some established vineyards grubbing up original vines to plant just the three traditional fizz varietals of *Chardonnay*, *Pinot Noir* and *Pinot Meunier*, and many brand new vineyards planting nothing but these (some on a huge scale). So why is English and Welsh wine doing so well?

Terroir

Studies by geologists interested in wine discovered that, particularly along the South and North Downs of southern England (and extending as far as Devon and Cornwall), the landscape shares many qualities with the Champagne region of France. Similarities have been noted in the composition of the rocks and soils, the topography, climate (particularly the number of sunshine hours) and even micro-climate, all of which make up the somewhat mystical quality

5

encapsulated by the French in the term *Terroir*. To recognise that areas of southern England potentially share the same *terroir* as Champagne was an astonishing revelation, and one that has helped propel the fledgling English wine industry forward at speed. And it's not just fizz. England and Wales produce the full gamut of *still* wines - red, white and pink and even an occasional late harvest dessert wine. I honestly think there is nothing finer than a drop of English wine, with names like *Bacchus*, *Ortega* or *Reichensteiner*, grape varietals originally developed in Germany but now quintessentially English. But I digress.

Bodium Castle Vineyard, East Sussex

Growing Grapes in Great Britain

Having already started to fall in love with wine itself, I also started to fall in love with the way it was created, from the techniques employed to grow vines, to what always appeared to me as the *Dark Magics* or mystical alchemy involved in transforming grape juice to the

So It Begins

wonderfully interesting drink we know as wine. Outside of the bottle, I also loved the aesthetics of the vineyard - the regimented order of the vines, the warmth of the summer sun on my back as I wandered (family in tow) up and down the vines of a vineyard somewhere in Kent or Sussex and even as far afield as Monmouth and the Brecon Beacons in Wales. Then it dawned on me. If people can grow grapes in the UK and these grapes can be turned into gorgeous tasting wine, then why  can't I do it? So began a challenge that to this day I'm still enjoying, a challenge and experience that I want to share with you.

I bought my first grapevine just after we moved into our marital home in southeast London. This was prior to me gaining any sort of in-depth knowledge about vines and I recall it was bought on a whim from a garden centre as is often the case with my plant purchases from garden centres. The grape varietal was called *Ortega* which I'd never heard of before, but I thought I would give it a go. I planted it without much ceremony in our garden next to a fence where we have quite a warm sun trap for the best part of the day and hoped it wouldn't die. It didn't and is still thriving today. My interest in growing grapes then steadily grew.

My first grapevine

With family still in tow, we would combine our assorted weekend days out to some Kentish medieval castle or Sussex farm with a little detour to a local vineyard. Soon, an excursion to an English vineyard even became the focus of the weekend outing, with the tank museum or petting zoo the thing we went to see *after* a visit to the vineyard.

The Urban Vineyard

We would often take ourselves on a self guided tour and by that I mean nosing around the vine lines, seeing how they were trellised and measuring how far apart vines had been planted etc. I started reading books about vine growing, the wheres and whys and hows, and then seeing how the techniques were employed in the vineyards we visited.

To develop our palettes, Mrs Olding (wife not mother) and I signed up for a course or two of wine tasting. Here we were introduced to the wines and grapes of the Old and New World, how to taste wine, how to enjoy it, and how to get something more from it than "...Mmm that's nice...". Now I'm certainly not a wine buff (or wine bore) - if it's "...whiff of tomcat..." or other such peculiar abstractions you're interested in, best seek advice elsewhere. I reckon there are many more years needed to refine my palette to extrapolate such intricate (and possibly a tad pompous) detail. However, what I *have* become is an enjoyer of wine and someone who's interested in how you create this complex and fascinating beast.

Ridgeview Wine Estate, East Sussex

So It Begins

The other thing I did was enroll on a course at the brilliant and pioneering agricultural college at Plumpton near Lewes in East Sussex. At the time of writing, this is the only place you can study the art and techniques of the Vintner and Vigneron in Britain, offering everything from evening classes, intensive crash courses (which is what I took), even a smashing Bachelor of Science degree in Oenology and assorted post graduate courses.

Along with the college course, over time, I gained a solid foundation knowledge drawn from books and the internet (book titles and internet links listed at the end of this book), plus countless conversations with vineyard owners (in the UK and abroad) at their vineyards or at various farming or wine events. Slowly but surely I felt at last I was able to start thinking about creating my own vineyard. And where better and more convenient to set up my fledgling enterprise/hobby, than in the urban environment.

View from the South Downs Way, East Sussex. Look hard enough and you should be able to see Plumpton College, Britain's Centre of Excellence in Wine education, training and research

The Urban Vineyard

2. Urban Spaces

So I already had the single *Ortega* grapevine growing well in my back garden. With my growing viticultural knowledge, I had started to manage its leafy canopy and prevent it from single-handedly taking over the entire corner of the garden it grew in, a task which continues to this day. I looked at the possibility of planting some more vines in the back garden, which is what I did in time, and creating an urban vineyard in your back garden is something I will return to throughout this book. But I had bigger plans than just my backyard.

Urban growing spaces are everywhere, but admittedly, not all are suitable or even sensible places to grow grapevines. Many local councils are now bringing horticultural colour and life to our public parks and roundabouts, sometimes installing raised flower beds along our high streets and inside our shopping malls. Plus there are the *Guerrilla Gardeners* who go out and secretly seed pretty much any bare ground to bring life to otherwise neglected mud - their motto: "...to fight the filth with forks and flowers...". Growing vines and setting up an urban vineyard needs careful planning and a serious commitment in the long term, but it doesn't necessarily need a whole lot of space.

Gardens & Community Spaces

Urban gardens offer many opportunities for growing grapevines, whether planting one or two along a sunlit fence or training one over an arbour. Vines will also grow in large pots on a patio, or on a sun-blessed balcony or roof terrace, as long as it's not too windy. But what about other urban spaces? How about school grounds, along a church wall, or in a bright office atrium? Well managed, I think a grapevine is just as pretty and aesthetically pleasing as a rose bush or flowering shrub, plus you get the chance to make a bottle or two of wine from its fruit.

Another possible avenue you might want to explore is unused or disused council land. I have known a number of local councils handing over small plots of land (usually protected from building development) to assorted community groups for the purposes of growing stuff (and horticultural beautification), helping to add a bit of colour to the urban jungle. Provided you have the freehold or permission to grow, plus I would say at least a 15 - 20 year lease, such plots could be ideal for establishing a small community urban vineyard. But there is one other type of urban space which works really well for a vineyard and that is an allotment.

Allotments

Ever since I had known my wife (high school sweethearts), I knew her dad had something called an *Allotment*. Allotments have been around for hundreds of years, possibly even dating back to Anglo-Saxon times. The idea originally involved a piece of land rented to the 'Labouring Poor' that was to be used to grow things for self consumption. Allotments are not unique to the UK and occur all across Europe and the USA (where they are sometimes known as *Community Gardens*). In 1908, the Small Holdings and Allotments Act was passed in the UK making it a duty of all local authorities to provide sufficient allotments according to need. In WW1, there were 1.5 million allotments in the UK, increasing to an all time peak of 1.75 million plots during WW2 and the famed *Dig for Victory* campaign.

Since that time there has been a gradual decline, resting today at around 300,000 plots. I discovered that the size of these plots can vary tremendously, from around 50m² to 250m², but they're never generally talked about in metric dimensions and always quoted in an archaic measurement based on something called a *Pole* or a *Rod*, with a square rod being 30¼ square yards. As a child of the 1970s and 80s (and an unapologetic metric-phile), I have no real notion of what a rod is, suffice to say that a square rod is 25.29m². But I digress.

I didn't know much about allotments and for many years (whilst courting my eventual wife to be) I did not take much interest in her dad's allotment at all, other than to eat the assorted produce that came from it either at lunch or dinner at the in-laws or through direct consumption of any surplus fruit and veg provided to us when they regularly popped round. My wife has oft talked about how, as children, she and her sister had accompanied their dad to his allotment to happily while away a Saturday afternoon playing amongst the cabbages. To be honest, I wasn't even sure what an allotment was nor what one looked like. During my childhood, my family had never mentioned such things, which is not to say we didn't grow stuff. There was always a small veggie patch in our garden, but nothing as regimented or organised as an allotment.

The Urban Vineyard

As the notion of trying to grow grapevines started to ferment in my mind (potentially on a scale larger than that afforded by my back garden), I spoke to my father-in-law and was duly invited over to see his plot. He is number 17 of 17 of the St  Mildred's Road Allotments, just off the South Circular in the suburban town of Lee, in the London Borough of Lewisham, SE12. Having never seen an allotment before I was unsure what to expect.

The individual plots on the site are (I later discovered) quite small compared to some other sites, with each measuring about 7m - 8m (23ft) wide and around 14m (45ft) long (I really have no idea what that amounts to in *Poles* or *Rods*). My father-in-law's plot was spectacular. Raspberries (or actually tayberries) and blackberries, leeks and tomatoes, butternuts, peas and beans. This was 20 odd years of hard graft and it showed. We walked along to check out the other plots and it became immediately apparent that his one was a rather prized affair. Indeed he has won the allotment of the year award for our borough. At that time, there were several plots that were

 untended and overgrown on the site, and a couple in assorted states of abandonment. It didn't take me long to realise that here before me was a potential vineyard waiting to happen. As I had learnt from my wine lessons, not all vineyards are multi-hectare, large scale enterprises, with many French vignerons tending very tiny plots. I told my father-in-law that I would very much like a plot and my name was added to the allotment waiting list.

Urban Spaces

The St Mildred's Road Allotments, Lewisham, London

Allotment waiting lists are something of a contentious issue in the UK. In recent years, ever since the re-awakening in Britain of the *Grow Your Own* ethos, waiting lists (in some London boroughs at least) have grown to such an extent, you are unlikely to get your hands on a plot for the next 20 years or so. According to the UK Allotment Association, at the time of writing there are currently over 90,000 people still on waiting lists. In many cases the only way a new person gets a plot is when the former holder dies. The demand for allotments is so great nowadays that councils are being asked to find new land to establish new plots. The National Trust is even setting aside land on some of their estates to provide growing space to those who want to start growing. Fortunately, the time I put my name down happened to be just ahead of said resurgence of interest in the art of 'allotmenteering', and to be honest, I had a fair bit of luck thrown my way.

The Urban Vineyard

As far as I can recall, ahead of me on the list were just a couple of other people. There was one lady who did not want a whole plot but possibly a more manageable half plot, which she was given. Someone else higher up the waiting list wanted to hold out for a particular plot, one that the existing tenant was going to be officially asked to vacate for not tending it as per the strict rules of the tenancy agreement all plot holders have to sign and adhere to. Quite a few other people on the list were offered an abandoned, overgrown plot but each turned it down as it was quite boggy and needed a lot of work to turn it back into land for growing. It was this sorry looking plot which then found its way to my position on the waiting list. The other current allotmenteers were aware of my plan to try and grow grapes and said this particular plot (number 11) was a no no, suffering from poor drainage. But I was determined to proceed. I felt I had the skills and knowledge and wherewithal to make my soggy plot of weedy, overgrown, neglected land into a glorious urban vineyard and so plot 11 became mine.

Plot 11 - The start of my Urban Vineyard

3. Preparing the Ground

Altitude

One factor I need to mention before we continue this journey together (as it could seriously affect your plans) is something that has (over the last decade or so) emerged as a key ingredient for successfully growing grapevines in the UK, and that is the height of the land above sea level. As far as grapevines are concerned, Britain is referred to as having 'marginal' growing conditions, with relatively short growing seasons. The minimum temperature for vine growth is 10° Celsius. Getting vines to grow, flourish and bear fruit which then ripen enough to make decent wine requires warmth, and at elevations beyond 150m (500ft) ASL (above sea level), I'm afraid you will struggle in the UK. Indeed, talking to viticulture consultants, they now say that 100m (330ft) ASL is the ceiling, reduced further to 50m (160ft) for certain varietals. It's possible that in an enclosed back garden, you might be able to counter a lower temperature (from being at a higher altitude) by exploiting a heat trap, but above 150m altitude out on a open plot of land, whilst you will still be able to grow grapevines, you will struggle to make nice wine from the grapes.

If your location is too high, I would have to recommend against trying to set up an urban vineyard, at least not without some sort of greenhouse or poly tunnel. To find the height of your land, you can look it up on the Ordinance Survey map system, or there are free altitude apps for your smart phone which is what I use. My plot sits at a very healthy 26m above sea level.

Frost, Wind and Sunshine

Three other things to consider when thinking about establishing your urban vineyard are risk of frost, amount of wind exposure and access to sunshine. Being in the urban (as opposed to the more chilly rural) environment, we do benefit from what is known as urban heat sink effects. First investigated in the early 1800s, curious Victorians discovered that cities are warmer than the countryside surrounding them, mostly down to heat-emitting human activity and the fact that urbanised areas are great storage heaters, absorbing heat during the day (all those black bitumen roads and concrete pavements), then releasing it later at night. Given that temperature is a key ingredient in grape growing, this is great. However, frost can still be an issue, not during the winter when the vines are fast asleep (vines are fine down to -15°C), but come Springtime. We've had some very weird Springs lately in the UK where there is a protracted heat spell (I once found myself in swim shorts on the beach near Margate in February), only to be followed by a severe cold snap. This can spell disaster. The early warmth will stimulate your vines to wake up from their winter slumber. But as the brand new shoots emerge into the sunshine, a late frost will cruelly burn the shoots, causing them to wither and die.

Obviously don't go trying to set up a vineyard where you know frost pockets can occur. Short of closely monitoring the evening temperatures and perhaps having a small garden incinerator bin on hand to fire up and warm the cold night air (as is done across the wine growing world when frost threatens), I'm afraid to say you have to live with this risk of late frost and hope for the best. The urban heat sink effect will help immensely, as does traffic flow (keeps the air moving). Frost damage has greater effect on young vines in that it can kill them. Once your vines are established, should you have some frost damage, chances are it won't be too significant and so you may just lose the odd cane or two.

Frost burn on newly emerged shoots

Exposure to high winds can be a problem in the urban environment, particularly where the concrete jungle creates 'funnelling'. Now a gentle breeze is beneficial to your urban vineyard as it helps dry the leaf canopy and reduce unwelcome humidity. But too strong a wind and it will blow away all that useful accumulated heat out of your vineyard. In an enclosed garden you should be fine, but on a small plot or open land, you may want to consider installing some sort of wind break, such as a row of trees or a hedge.

Finally, sunshine. I read that it can take 1250 hours of sunshine for a grapevine to produce ripe fruit. Access to direct sunshine is important for many reasons, not just in providing warmth, but also for ripening, for a process called *Floral Initiation* (a process which determines the following year's crop - see Chapter 12), and for the vine's canes to mature. In short, if the sun is shining, you want it shining on your vines. The simple note here is to try to make sure your vines are not going to get shaded by any nearby trees or buildings.

Preparing the Soil

Preparing a small plot of land or an area in your back garden for growing vines all depends on what state you find said ground to begin with. For back garden urban vineyards, unless you've just moved house and taken on a garden that was left to go wild, getting a suitable site ready for grapevines should be fairly easy. First try to identify any sun traps - the vines will thank you for it. A site next to a south facing fence is preferable (the fence is very useful when it comes to establishing a support system or trellis - see Chapter 9), or you may have a pergola you want to grow a grapevine or two over. A quick word of warning - while pergolas and arbours and other garden structures look lovely draped in a grapevine, if the vine is forced to grow too much or left to run wild, and if the number of grape bunches isn't carefully controlled, then the grapes produced from what can become a large and often madly out of control vine are not necessarily going to be good for making wine. I'll talk more about this in Chapter 5 when we look at vineyard design, but suffice to say when I've been asked in the past to make wine from a huge *Triffid* type vine bearing vast amounts of grapes, the wine is never that nice. Prior to planting a vine in your garden, clear away any ground cover and any weeds at least 50cm (2ft) around the proposed site of each vine. For those taking on a feral overgrown garden or an allotment or other plot of land, a more significant challenge may await prior to planting.

Preparing the Ground

A well tended allotment or urban plot whose previous tenant worked the land, grew stuff and followed the rules laid down by their landlord or allotment association might need very little preparation work. I'm not sure about other allotment groups, but ours has a short written contract which lists out a set of rules you effectively agree to adhere to when taking on your plot. This is an attempt to keep the plots in good working order not just throughout your time as a tenant, but also when they get passed on. Reading the contract I had signed when awarded my plot, I noted that apparently the previous owner had promised to keep the plot in good nick, "...free of perennial weeds, with the edges clearly defined..." Sadly what I saw before me looked like a wasteland you might find at the back of an industrial estate. My plot had been untended for some years and had been left to return to nature. What I had agreed to take on was heavily overgrown by every weed possible, with bramble and other nasty stuff running the length of the site. There was no shed, no access paths, no beds, actually no bare soil at all. And when it rained, there were puddles.

My sorry looking plot

The state of your allotment (or garden bed) will obviously dictate how much graft you have to put in just to initiate a healthy and productive urban vineyard. One of the big things about vines is that preparation prior to planting is particularly important (try saying that after a glass of wine). It is absolutely well worth every second spent getting your site in order long before you buy your vines. I took on my plot in September with the knowledge I had six months to get it ready for planting the following Spring. In fact, starting preparation in the

Autumn prior to planting is a must. Set up your site well, and the vines will thrive. Rush into planting before the site is ready, and the vines may grow, but pretty soon they will fail and you will struggle to correct major problems later on down the line.

Grass & Weed Removal

Perceived wisdom for the establishment of a vineyard is to kill off all grass cover, right down to the roots. This would mean applying a herbicide, something I didn't want to do. You could cover your grassy land with old carpet or other dense matting to kill off the grass, but this takes quite a few months to be effective. Another option is simply slicing the grass off the soil. It turns out this might have been something a previous tenant of my allotment had done, as my current surface level was a bit lower than the plots either side - that and I discovered a big pile of rotted down soil just behind my plot, something that I later used to build up the level of the soil. I took the decision, rightly or wrongly, to simply plough the grass into the soil using a hired in rotavator. My thought here was that the grass would add to the nutrient base - but

I get the feeling I should have killed it off, as it has taken many years to get the weeds under control, and they still spring up.

Another job is to get rid of any large perennial weeds. While you can use a herbicide, the most effective way is to dig them out by hand as deep as possible to remove all the deep set roots. But what to do with all those weeds? I was on the understanding that I should compost all organic material, but then I had a worry that the seeds of these weeds are so tenacious, they might lie dormant in my compost, ready for me to unwittingly re-seed my plot with the weeds when, later on, I liberally add my homemade compost back to the soil. Any woody weeds and those that were identified as perennial (plus any others that looked a bit mean) were bagged up and escorted off the premises. But most of the soft green weeds found their way into one of three (yes three) compost bins that I set up at the back of my plot.

Compost Bins

Homemade wooden compost bins are fairly easy to build, and as a youth I did just that in the back of my parents' garden. Using the best DIY skills I could muster (aged 13), I constructed a cube-shaped receptacle out of old wooden slats, and lined the inside with narrow gauge chicken wire. I designed a nifty way to lift up the front panel (held within doweling rails) so I could extract the rotted down compost from the bottom of the pile. Many years later, and having taken charge of my new weedy and boggy allotment, I decided I would skip the DIY and just buy some big garden compost bins, especially ones that didn't even need any assembly. Our local council (the London Borough of Lewisham) is very good about recycling and composting and offered cheap priced, plastic compost bins which, when erected, look like mini Daleks from Dr Who. There are a wide variety of compost bins on the market, but I decided to go with cheap and cheerful over grandiose elegance – your compost bins are not

The Urban Vineyard

going to be a focus point of your urban vineyard so don't let them overplay their part. The key design feature is that you are able to put stuff in the top (grass cuttings, non perennial weeds, paper, cardboard, vegetable kitchen slops) and then some months later, access your rich, homemade compost soil from a hatch at the bottom.

Whether in your back garden or on a plot of land, I believe that compost bins are essential, not least so you can recycle any organic stuff you remove from the land and get some great soil in return. Without them, you would not only be removing nutrients from your plot, but you'd also have to find the time (and a location) to dispose of it all. Away from my allotment, our back garden has managed perfectly well with just the one compost bin, but for a small plot of land, I would definitely have two or three. Set your bins on level ground which has good access to the soil below, i.e. don't go placing them on a site you have nicely levelled with bricks or on a concrete base. The reason is that you want the worms (and other assorted beasties) naturally living in the soil to have easy access to the contents of your bins, as it's mostly their action which turns the various things you chuck in, into glorious homemade soil. The only other note is that when fully operational, your compost bins might smell (especially if you feed them with kitchen waste) and so I would locate them away from any prospective sitting areas.

Assessing Soil Structure

Before you think about planting vines, you need to consider what sort of soil you are planting them in and whether that soil needs adjusting or helping in any way. Soil chemistry for growing vines is an immensely complex subject and the focus of many an oenological PhD (and something I briefly return to in Chapter 12). I got the impression from various discussions abroad that many European wine growers are adamant that the makeup of the soil on which the vine is grown is absolutely vital to the resulting character of the wine. As far as I know this has still yet to be scientifically proven (i.e. does a gravelly/flinty substrate really confer a 'stony' flavour to the wine), but I did come to the conclusion that getting the right soil *structure* and *texture* is paramount to achieving a set of healthy and robust plants. That's not to say that nutrient levels aren't also very important (and something I will return to later), but at this stage of the game, it's time to get to know your soil structure. One simple way to assess what sort of soil you have is to follow the flow chart overleaf:

The Urban Vineyard

Soil Assessment

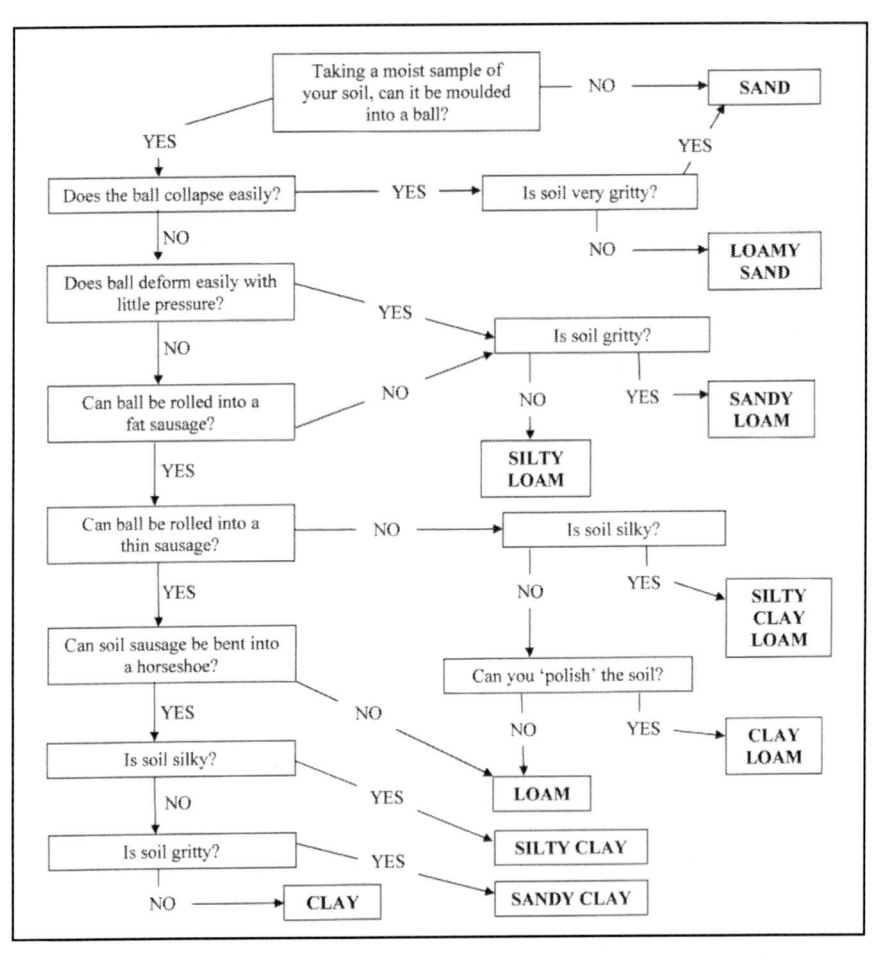

```
                    Taking a moist sample of
                    your soil, can it be moulded ——NO——▶  SAND
                         into a ball?
        YES                                      YES
         ▼                                        ▲
Does the ball collapse easily? ——YES——▶ Is soil very gritty?
         │
        NO                                  NO          LOAMY
         ▼                                   ────────▶  SAND
Does ball deform easily with
      little pressure?
         │                      YES
        NO                       ▼
         ▼                Is soil gritty?
Can ball be rolled into a ──NO──▶      NO    YES        SANDY
      fat sausage?                              ──────▶  LOAM
        YES                      ▼
         ▼                   SILTY
Can ball be rolled into a ──NO──▶  LOAM
      thin sausage?
        │                 Is soil silky?
       YES                  NO    YES                  SILTY
        ▼                                    ──────▶   CLAY
Can soil sausage be bent into                          LOAM
       a horseshoe?          ▼
        │               Can you 'polish' the soil?
       YES      NO         NO    YES                   CLAY
        ▼                                    ──────▶   LOAM
  Is soil silky?             ▼
       NO     YES         LOAM
        ▼
  Is soil gritty?       SILTY CLAY
       NO     YES
        ▼               SANDY CLAY
       CLAY
```

Source: Flow chart adapted (with permission) from course notes from the Intensive Principles of Vine Growing course, Plumpton College

One of the many passed-down wisdoms of viticulture is that grapevines don't like wet feet, so free draining soil is what you need. Not only that, but poorly drained soils are cooler and take longer to

Preparing the Ground

heat up come Springtime, and soggy soil can also restrict root growth. You may be lucky and have soil that boasts naturally good drainage, such as a nice sandy loam. But a cautionary note as you dance around on your splendid loam - a well drained soil may be great in regard to drainage, but it can have an impact on the soil's nutrient balances. What's good for the physical structure might actually work against the soil's chemical makeup and will need addressing when assessing soil nutrient balance.

The soil down our way in south-east London is very much London Clay. I was also burdened with the fact that the plot of land I had taken on was known to bear puddles after a heavy rainfall, suggesting very poor drainage - both factors not ideal. Before I did anything else, I felt I had to do everything in my power to optimise the physical quality of the soil and so started by addressing the issue of drainage. Yet my research threw up what appeared to be contradictory advice.

Improving Soil Texture

As with many factors on my journey to create an urban vineyard, improving soil drainage confused me. My lecturer on the intensive vine growing course I took at Plumpton College recommended the need for something called 'Sub Soiling'. This involves attaching to your tractor a device with metre long steel prongs which go deep into the ground and literally rip through the soil. Great for farms and large commercial vineyards, not so good for allotments or back gardens.

An alternative to breaking up the soil by physically ripping through it, is to add stuff to it that will naturally open up the structure of the soil, increasing spaces for water to drain away. Everything I read recommended adding two things - course builders' sand and rotted organic matter. When added to the soil and dug in as deep as possible, both should effectively open up the soil structure and thus allow greater water flow and improved drainage. I decided to add both. If you're thinking about planting vines in your back garden or in a patio pot, when preparing the soil, mix in a couple of shovelfuls of sand and some well rotted (two year) horse manure when forking it over. This should do the trick nicely. For a larger plot of land, you'll obviously need quite a bit more.

I duly ordered a metric tonne of builders' sand, but delivering it was a bit tricky. My allotment is located off a main road (the South Circular, en route to Catford) and is accessed by a narrow private road running along the back of a row of houses. Getting a flatbed delivery truck down the access road was always going to be tricky. The delivery arrived and the skilled driver managed to reverse half way down, but sadly could not get the whole way, so my tonne of sand was offloaded about 100m from my plot. I then had to manually transport the sand one wheelbarrow at a time, down the track to the site.

Now a tonne of sand might sound a lot, but it isn't actually that much, particularly when spread over the surface of an allotment measuring 7m by 13m. I felt its addition (dug into the soil) was more a token nod towards aiding drainage at this stage. Along with the sand, I also found on the web a company that delivered two year old

Preparing the Ground

rotted horse manure which would work perfectly as the organic matter component to help aid drainage. I ordered the minimum of 15 bags, again delivered by a truck that couldn't quite make it down the road to the plot, so some manual shifting was involved. The horse poo was then spread liberally over the land and again dug in. You can dig it in by hand, but I would suggest hiring a small rotavator.

Now here comes the start of many contradictions I encountered when setting up my urban vineyard. As far as I could see, adding rotted horse manure to soil destined to be a vineyard has two potentially *opposite* effects. The fibrous material provided by the poo should definitely open up the structure of my clay laden soil and help promote drainage. But the rich nutrients within the manure (particularly nitrogen) would add to the already rich nutrient base that existed in my soil. The former (drainage) was what I wanted, but the latter (increased nutrients) I didn't need at all (for reasons I'll explain later) and in fact wanted to restrict. Adding the rotted horse manure felt like a *Push Me Pull You* from Dr Doolittle.

If you're lucky and have good free draining soil, or you reckon the addition of some sand and rotted horse poo is all you will need to improve your soil structure and drainage, then feel free to jump ahead to Chapter 4 where I look at choosing your vines. If however you still have a bit of a boggy plot of land bearing soggy soil after rain, or you're just intrigued as to what I did next, then please read on. Like me, you might need to consider installing a DIY drainage system.

Installing a DIY Drainage System

Given the original poor state of my allotment and the knowledge that vines really do not like wet feet, my drive to improve the drainage on my plot went a step further. To help alleviate the immediate threat of water logging, soon after acquiring the site, my father-in-law had taken it upon himself to dig a trench on either side of my plot, a spade width wide and a spade width deep, to see if we could somehow drain the plot of its excess water. Come the rains the following February (2008), these trenches rapidly filled with water. Lo and behold, the water did appear to be draining out of the soil into the trenches. My plot was definitely getting drier and puddles were no longer forming on the surface. However, the water collecting in the side trenches wasn't just draining out of *my* plot. On closer inspection, I noticed little streams of water flowing into the trenches as runoff from plots 1 through 10 (I am plot 11) located just slightly uphill (and upstream) to me. I knew my plot was inherently boggy, but it was now clear this wasn't being helped by water draining from the adjacent plots. The location and design of the current drainage trenches was also not an entirely workable solution, leading to issues of health and safety, and more than once my feet got soaked following a slip into the water filled troughs.

A bit of an internet session later and I came across a possible solution. I unearthed some plans showing how farmers or sportsfield grounds staff could construct a full scale drainage system. There were several different designs, so I picked one I thought most suited the size and needs of my plot and decided to try and install a scaled down DIY version.

Materials & Design

First I had to get hold of some sort of 'membrane' material that would be used to line a set of drainage channels. This would stop any plants trying to force their fibrous roots into what would become a transient water reservoir. Then I had to get some special perforated drainage tubing. I found this at my local hardware store, but was initially confused as to the girth I would require. Too small and it might not work. Too big and I might as well be trying to drain a premier league football pitch. I decided on something in the middle ground 60mm (2½in) wide, colour coded blue, and purchased 25m (82ft), enough to run the length of a channel down each side of my plot. The third constituent of the drainage system was pea gravel. I ordered a tonne which got delivered at the very end of the access road to the plots and so had to be shifted by me and the father-in-law by hand, one wheelbarrow at a time.

Now my design (cribbed from the interweb) involved digging two parallel trenches on either side of my plot, so I used the trenches we'd already dug, making them a little wider and a little deeper. I then laid the membrane material into the trench (to line it), adding a layer of gravel to the bottom to hold it in place. Next I laid the specialist perforated blue drainage pipe into the membrane-lined trench and shoveled in more gravel, effectively burying the pipe within a matrix of the pea sized gravel. To finish off, I folded over the membrane material poking out the top of each trough, loading on a final thin layer of gravel to hold it all down. As expected, one tonne of gravel was not enough, so I had to order a second tonne of gravel for the second channel to complete the job.

Drainage Channel Design
(cross section view)

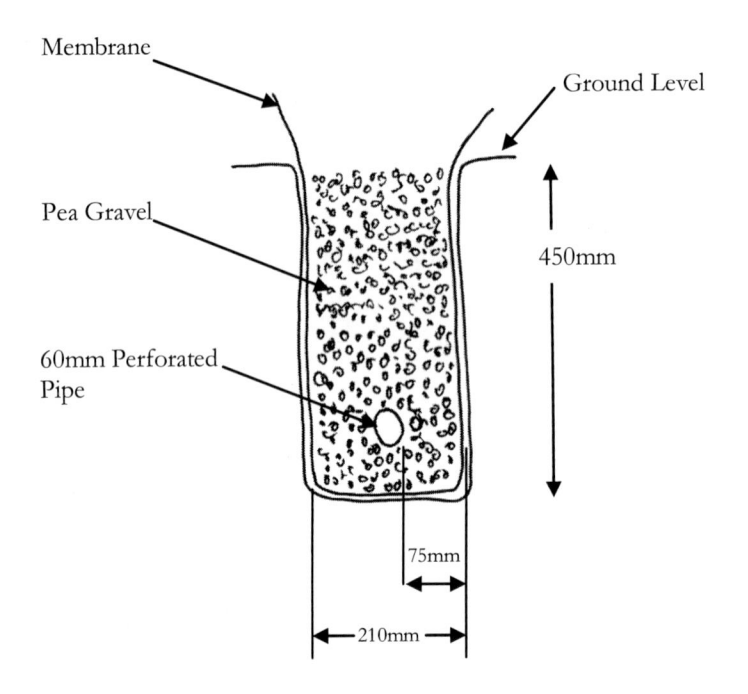

- Membrane
- Pea Gravel
- 60mm Perforated Pipe
- Ground Level
- 450mm
- 75mm
- 210mm

So I had a means for the soil on my plot to drain itself, and I also had a way to capture any subsoil water running off from higher ground, diverting it away from my plot. What I needed now was twofold - a way to link the two drainage channels installed along either side of my plot (to create a single interconnected drainage system), plus, and this bit is critical, a way to vent the water that would accumulate in my DIY drainage system.

To solve the first issue I simply purchased a length of wide diameter drainage pipe, the stuff I expect you might use (if of course 'you' were a plumber) in some sort of household drain installation, as

Preparing the Ground

opposed to the skinnier pipes that are used to take water down from roof guttering. Then I simply dug a ditch along the short side at the front of my plot, and lowered in the pipe to link together the two long drainage channels. So now the drainage system was one continuous, three sided, interconnected unit. Working out an effective way to then remove the water from the system was a tad more complicated.

**Aerial View of
my Drainage System**

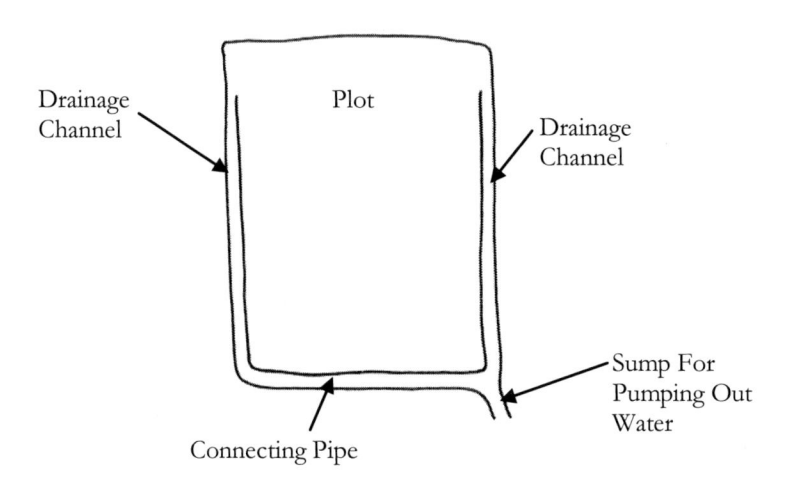

Drainage Channel

Plot

Drainage Channel

Sump For Pumping Out Water

Connecting Pipe

The internet designs had the 'exhaust' of their drainage systems simply exiting at a lower point downhill, allowing any water to drain away to lower ground. Perfect. The plan in my case was to drain the water onto the concrete access road that runs alongside the allotments - but there was a problem. The vent of my three sided drainage system turned out to be around 30cm (1ft) *below* the level of the road. As the February and March rains gently filled my now fully operational drainage system, there was no way to expel the water. This was obviously not good - as soon as the system filled up with water, it could no longer function to effectively drain any further soakage. What I needed was a way to pump the water out of the system.

Venting the Water

The solution came in the form of a simple, hand operated, bilge pump that you might use on a boat (found once again with a Google search). This device looks like a sort of bicycle pump, only it sucks water up at the bottom and blows it out near the top. Now when my drainage system has standing water in it, I just pop the pump into what is effectively my *exit* sump and pump the water out onto the concrete road where it drains away. Once the sump is empty, I leave it for 20 minutes (whilst I go off and attend to other needs), whereby any additional excess water drains out from the soil and refills the drainage system. Then I pump it out again from the sump. So with a bit of knowledge gleaned from the net, a bit of modification and some creativity, I created a functional drainage system for my plot. And it worked (and still does). Gone was the boggy patch of scrubland, replaced by a dry, free-draining clay loam soil, all ready to establish my urban vineyard.

Now while you're busy working through the Autumn and Winter months trying to get your soil ready for your vines, you have to think about actually ordering your vines.

4. Choosing Your Vines

Once you've identified an area in your garden and cleared a space for some vines, or you're in the process of getting your plot of land or allotment in good order, you need to be thinking about what vines you would like to grow and plan how you're going to plant them. This could be as simple a decision as seeing what your local garden centre (or vineyard) has for sale. Just make sure you buy a wine grape (as opposed to a dessert grape) if it is wine you intend to make. One of the English vineyards we regularly go to (Denbies in Surrey) has quite a range of grapevines on offer in their plant shop, including many immediately recognisable varietals such as *Chardonnay* or *Pinot Noir*. These are robust, healthy plants, well established, and great if you just want a vine or two to grow in the garden. I bought a fabulous Pinot Noir from them for the garden and it's still growing well. But packaged and potted up like this, they don't come cheap, and you'll be looking at around £10 - £14 a plant.

If you have grander plans than just one or two vines, then I would suggest a different course of action and that is to order direct from a vine nursery. While considerably cheaper (about £2 per vine), this course of action comes with additional choices and further levels of complexity, plus you usually need to place your order in the November/December prior to planting the following Spring. Choosing vines and planning your urban vineyard is quite a thoughtful process, fraught with 'what ifs' and needs great consideration for the future. There are so many separate and yet interconnected decisions to be made and I will take each one in turn.

Many people will refer to a grape *variety* (and indeed you'll find the word *variety* splashed across the wine internet), but apparently the more correct term is *varietal* (aka *cultivar*). I was told by a learned wine instructor "...strictly speaking, they should not be referred to as *varieties*, because they do not 'breed true' unlike Spaniels, which are a *variety* of dog..." So there you go.

As well as the actual varietal(s) of grapevine you might want, for the dedicated urban vigneron ordering direct from a vine nursery, there is also the rootstock to consider (see below). As part of your ordering process, you will also need to know how many vines to order and so you will need to consider how far apart you're going to plant

Choosing Your Vines

them and if you are establishing several lines of vines, what distance to keep between the lines (width of the *alleys* - see Chapter 5). Even at this early stage of your planning, you also need to consider the system of vine support you will install (the trellis system - Chapter 9) and how you will manage the canopy (Chapter 11). All these factors will be covered in depth later on, but you need to have all these thoughts in the back of your head right from the start. One thing I hope you can do with this book is jump back and forth - there's no point me jumping around too much within each chapter, otherwise it will get way too confusing. But as and when you feel the need to jump about, you go on right ahead.

Grape Varietals

Your choice of grape *varietal* or *cultivar* (as is the more trendy word at the moment) is dependent on a number of factors, not least what sort of wine you want to make. But before you go rushing out and ordering the classic French types (many now available from suppliers) hoping to create a robust bottle of Pinot Noir or a chewy oaked Chardonnay, there are several significant factors to consider. First, some grapevines are not necessarily the most suitable (or easiest) to grow in Britain's climate (often referred to as a 'cool climate' as far as viticulture is concerned) and many can be quite difficult to get to flourish (particularly for making still wines). Back with the pioneers of English wine, varietals chosen were mostly derived from Germany, including names like Müller-Thurgau, Seyval Blanc, Madeleine Angevine and Triomphe d'Alsace. These varietals can still be seen in the older vineyards of southern Britain, yet for the urban vigneron they too pose a problem.

Some of the most popular grape varietals from the Old and New World need considerable chemical spraying over the course of the growing year in order to control the likes of Downy and Powdery mildews and Botrytis (see Chapter 12). Infection by mildews drastically reduces the volume of fruit produced by each vine, and infection is more prevalent in damp warm climates, as opposed to dryer climates, as it's the moist air which encourages such rots. Spraying is not just costly but involves specific equipment (you don't need a tractor for a small urban vineyard, but you may still need a backpack-mounted, hand delivery system). Plus there are also your neighbours to consider who aren't going to be too happy about your anti-fungal spray drifting across their vegetables or garden lawns. Now it is possible to find 'organic' spray solutions, such as the famous Bordeaux Mixture (a mixture of copper sulphate and slaked lime) invented in the late 19th century unsurprisingly in the Bordeaux region of France. But again, spray drift, expense and the fact you have to spray regularly throughout most of the growing season adds a considerable burden and use of any spray requires training. But there is an alternative.

Interspecific Hybrids

One solution for the urban vigneron is to consider choosing what are known as interspecific hybrid varietals. Many varietals or cultivars are actually *intra* specific hybrids (including all the German names listed opposite) which are biological crosses *within* a species. What I'm talking about here is a cross between two *different* species giving an *inter* specific hybrid. In England, these come in the form of crosses between native American vine species and a selection of German varietals. The reason why these interspecific hybrids are so good for the allotment or garden vigneron is that they have inbuilt natural defence against mildew infection and rarely (if ever) need spraying. Native American species by themselves tend to produce grapes with poor quality juice and as a result, make nasty wine, but they have very good disease resistance and are heavy croppers. By biologically crossing these American species with European species to create interspecific hybrids, clever oenological scientists in Germany came up with a way for us to benefit from the positive character traits provided by the American vines while still creating quality wine.

The choice for these disease resistant interspecific hybrid varietals is limited, but there is a choice none the less. Before choosing my vines, I read up on all the different possibilities and came up with a shortlist of three for my vineyard, two white and one red. For the whites I chose hybrid varietals called *Phoenix* and *Orion* and for the red, a grape called *Regent*. The names might not be familiar to you (at the moment), but as far as new plantings for English and Welsh still wines, these are in the premiere division. Phoenix is a cross between Bacchus (itself a hybrid between Silvaner, Riesling and Müller-Thurgau) and Seyve Villard, and Orion is a cross between something called Optima and Seyve Villard. Regent is a hybrid of varietals called Diana (Silvaner x Müller-Thurgau) and Chamboucin. All these hybrids were engineered in Germany beginning in the 1960s, by a chap called Prof Alleweldt working at the Geilweilerhof Institute, finally being released for cultivation in the 1990s.

Of course you could still choose from a multitude of (non interspecific) *Vitis vinifera* varietals (e.g. Ortega, Huxelrebe, Dornfelder to name but three more from Germany or the classic Chardonnay or Pinot Noir from France), but these will all need a dedicated regime of spraying. My plan was to have two rows of Phoenix (reportedly to be a bit Sauvignon Blanc in character), one row of Orion (more a spicy aromatic Chenin Blanc style), and then one row of Regent (Cabernet Sauvignon style). To be honest and drawing on my experience of tasting English reds (some of which went down like drinking sandpaper), I had no great hopes for the Regent grapes to make great red wine, but I thought I would give them a go.

When I started out, you wouldn't see interspecific hybrid

Choosing Your Vines

vines on sale in garden centres due to the simple fact that the average visitor wouldn't recognise the names and so wouldn't buy them. Just yesterday I glanced at the latest horticultural supplies catalogue that came in the post and blow me down if there's a Phoenix and a Regent grapevine for you to buy.

To create an urban vineyard, or at least to have enough fruit to be able to make a few bottles of wine, I would suggest you need a minimum of five plants (of the same type). Rather than source from a garden centre, I decided to buy direct from a supplier, but if you do that, you will be asked what rootstock you want.

Rootstock

Back in the nineteenth century, a tiny aphid-like creature called *Phylloxera,* which was originally native to North America, was inadvertently introduced to France. This little beastie caused widespread destruction in the vineyards of Europe, particularly attacking the roots (and sometimes the leaves) of the grapevines. Unlike American *Vitis* species who had evolved natural defences against phylloxera, the European *Vitis vinifera* was susceptible to attack. To this day there is no cure for a phylloxera attack, but resistance is now forged by grafting a phylloxera resistant American rootstock onto the European vines. Grafting is completely different to hybridization - what's neat about this, is that the rootstock does not interfere with the development of the European grapes, and you can also choose different rootstocks to match your specific soil conditions.

There were around ten rootstocks available when I went to buy my vines (even more now I believe), and each one is suited to certain soil types and certain growing conditions. There are some that are good for soils with high fertility, low fertility, high calcium etc. The most common root stock is called SO4 (not sure why) but others include 5BB, 125AA and 5C. The only way to know what rootstock is best for your soil is to know your soil. You can find this out by sending a sample off for a soil analysis - the results will also be important if you need to adjust specific nutrient levels in your soil to better help your vines (see Chapter 12).

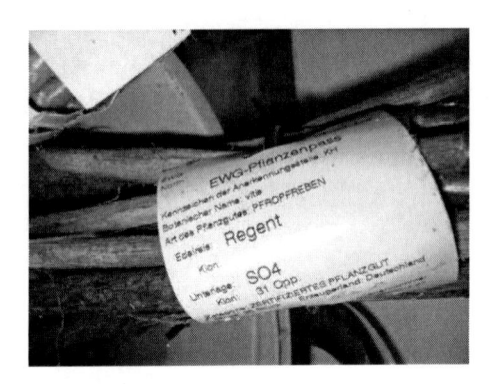

Regent vines with SO4 rootstock

Soil Analysis

A quick web search revealed a number of places to send my soil and for around £20, I got quite a thorough breakdown. When preparing a sample of your soil to send away, try to take a number of samples (even across a small plot). Dig down at least two spade depths (to the subsoil strata), plus take a sample of the top soil, but don't include any grass or vegetation. Then give all your sub samples a thorough mixing before sending off the required amount (usually at least 500g) for analysis. My plot came back as high in phosphorus (needed for plants to fix energy), potassium (needed for ripening) and magnesium (essential for chlorophyll formation), all good news for my vines. It also registered fairly high in nitrogen which is to be expected from an allotment.

Choosing Your Vines

The other thing a soil analysis can give you is a measure of the acidity or alkaline level of your soil, indicated via the pH scale. A soil that is acid has a pH value lower than 7, neutral is pH 7, and alkaline is greater than 7. The soil pH is a key component in growing vines and determines how well your vines can take up other nutrients. Mine came in at pH 7.18. Fortunately this is perfect as the recommendation for vines is a soil pH between 6.5 - 7.5. If your soil is too alkaline (pH greater than 8), it's actually quite hard to lower the pH, but you could try adding something like ferrous sulphate to increase acidity. A soil that is too acid (pH lower than pH 6) and you can add lime (crushed limestone) to make it more alkaline. I would suggest seeking additional advice (from a friendly garden centre) if you are trying to alter the pH of your plot and accurately follow the instructions as to how much of a substance you need to add to raise/lower the pH of your soil by the right amount.

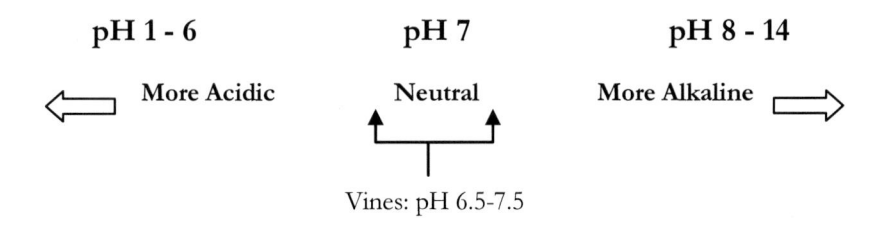

pH 1 - 6	pH 7	pH 8 - 14
⟵ More Acidic	Neutral	More Alkaline ⟶

Vines: pH 6.5-7.5

Once you have the results from your soil analysis, you can then seek advice from a commercial vine supplier as to the correct rootstock for your vines to best match your soil profile. For example, if you have chalky soil, you would need to have a chalk tolerant rootstock etc. Based on my soil analysis, the most suitable rootstock for my soil turned out to be the common SO4 type which is suitable for a wide range of soil types (but especially clay soils) and it can also help to combat excess vigour (which was likely to be the case given the high nitrogen content of my soil). Apparently the SO4 rootstock can have problems taking up magnesium from the soil which is something I later discovered to be very true (see Chapter 12).

Buying vines in bulk is fairly easy now we are in the midst of the English wine Renaissance. I found several companies (via the web) that could supply my chosen vine varietals (with associated rootstock), however only one could supply them in the small numbers I needed. Most have a 50 or 100 unit minimum per grape varietal, and the size and scale of my proposed urban vineyard meant I needed the flexibility of buying a lot less. But before you put in your order, you need to work out how many vines you want and to do that, you need to decide on the design and layout of your prospective vineyard.

5. Urban Vineyard Design

Allegedly you require 1.13kg (2.5lbs) of grapes to make a bottle of wine. For the back garden vigneron, I would say you need at least 3 - 5 vines of the same grape varietal to produce enough fruit to make at least a demijohn or two of wine (one demijohn becomes 6 bottles or thereabouts). Sadly at this small scale, the impact of natural wastage you incur during the wine creation process (see Chapter 13 onwards) is far greater than if you are making wine on a larger scale.

Grapevines in the Garden

When assessing your garden as to potential locations for grapevines, the key is having some vertical space for the vine to grow up and a clear view of a (hopefully) sunny sky. Ideally you want a south facing wall or fence nestling in a little sun trap, protected from the wind. But a word of warning - as I've mentioned earlier, many vines that I've seen growing in various back gardens look very pretty and add a certain Mediterranean feel to the setting, especially winding round an arbour, but most of these are useless if the owner wanted to make nice drinkable wine from their fruit. The problem is the size of the vine and the sheer volume of fruit it has been allowed to produce. I have seen single vines that have run riot, growing here, there and everywhere, producing copious amounts of poor quality fruit. Vines that are grown with the intention of making wine need to be controlled, managed and very much restricted in their growth in order to balance the amount of fruit produced against the amount of foliage (leaves and canes). I'll return to this later when we look at canopy management in Chapter 11.

The Urban Vineyard

An individual vine doesn't need a whole bag of room, but you don't want to have it crowded in by other plants. Also make sure it is located in the warmest, sunniest part of your garden. My own garden faces roughly south west so it gets a goodly amount of sunshine, but because of some large trees in our neighbours' gardens, there's considerable shading at the far end. The suntraps occur nearer the house and this is where the vines flourish. I now have six vines in the garden, in effect creating two lines of vines, one running down each fence of our oblong back yard.

Urban Vineyard Design

The great thing about grapevines in a garden is that they can grow at the back of flower borders, with wire supports secured into fence posts (more on this in Chapter 9). If you plan to establish an urban vineyard in your garden, the thing to consider at this stage is simply how far apart to plant your vines, as this will dictate how many you can fit in. Distance between vines is explored in more detail below, but I would say they should be at least 1.5m - 2m (5ft - 7ft) apart, because if your flower beds are anything like ours, the vine will be competing with all manner of shrubs and bushes etc for nutrients and light. Planting your vines is covered in Chapter 7 and installing a trellis in Chapter 9.

Vineyard Design for an Allotment

Out on an open plot of land or on an allotment, vineyard design is a bit more complicated. Here you won't be relying on a fence to support your vines, and will need to install a free standing trellis system to hold them up and train them along (see Chapter 9). As I have said before, to establish an urban vineyard, you have to plan ahead and think through many of the future stages in the life of your vineyard. This will ensure any actions taken now don't screw up the bigger picture later on! For example, when you are considering potential vineyard design (at this stage, simply to know how many vines to order), there are three main factors to ponder - orientation of your vine rows, the space between the vines within each row, and the space between the rows (aka alley width).

The Urban Vineyard

Vineyard Orientation

Every other plot on my south London allotment is laid out in traditional style with beds running width ways across the plots. This is how the books suggest you do it, because it allows ease of access to each bed, particularly if you divide up your allotment with paths. But it would be daft to run vine lines width ways across my plot as I would end up with lots of short, silly looking rows, all ends and not much in the middle. I planned to completely break with allotment etiquette and plant my vines in rows running up and down the plot's length. Fortunately the position of the sun and the orientation of the planet was working with me here.

I'm lucky in that my allotment is south facing and being south facing, it was ideal for my proposed urban vineyard design. By planning to have my rows running North - South (as opposed to East - West), each vine would get the maximum amount of sunshine throughout the day, starting on one side in the morning and crossing over to the other in the afternoon. Now if your plot is not South facing, or if the orientation does not allow a North - South planting, there's nothing stopping you planting East - West. Indeed there's some evidence to suggest this may have its own unique advantages. With an East - West orientation, you get more sunlight on the vines in the Spring and Autumn (as opposed to a midsummer maximum with North - South). Plus the vines get maximum light coverage at midday (which for North - South lines it is at a minimum, with the sun directly overhead). Whichever way you orient your vine lines, having long accessible rows with day long access to sunshine is key.

Urban Vineyard Design

Vine Spacing & Soil Fertility

Next we come onto vine spacing. You will want your vines to be as close to each other as possible (so you can pack more in), but not so close they will detrimentally compete with each other for light and nutrients. I say 'detrimentally compete', but a bit of competition is not a bad thing as far as vines go. Underpinning just how close you can plant your vines is the fertility of your soil.

With a low fertile soil, you could plant grapevines within a metre (3ft) of each other. I've been to places (with quite a rocky substrate i.e. very low fertility) where the vines are planted incredibly close together. In this situation, as far as plant on plant competition goes, it's not such a great problem, as the vines never manage to grow big enough to shade or otherwise hinder each other with large foliage. With a healthy, mature allotment or back garden, you will almost certainly be sat at the other end of the spectrum and have soil screaming with fertility. Many allotments have been around for decades, and for decades, allotmenteers have been plying the soil with all matter of manure and nutrients. As I said in Chapter 4, when I took on my plot in southeast London, I did the scientific thing and got my soil sampled by a soil analysis lab. The results, even for my unkempt, unloved, overgrown plot was a soil rich in nutrients and as it happened, well balanced with the various elements measured. The trouble I faced with regard to establishing an urban vineyard was having soil with too much fertility (indicated by high levels of nitrogen) - this in turn directly feeds back into the question in hand of how far apart you should plant your vines (which will then tell you how many vines you will plant) - it's a bit circular but then that's viticulture!

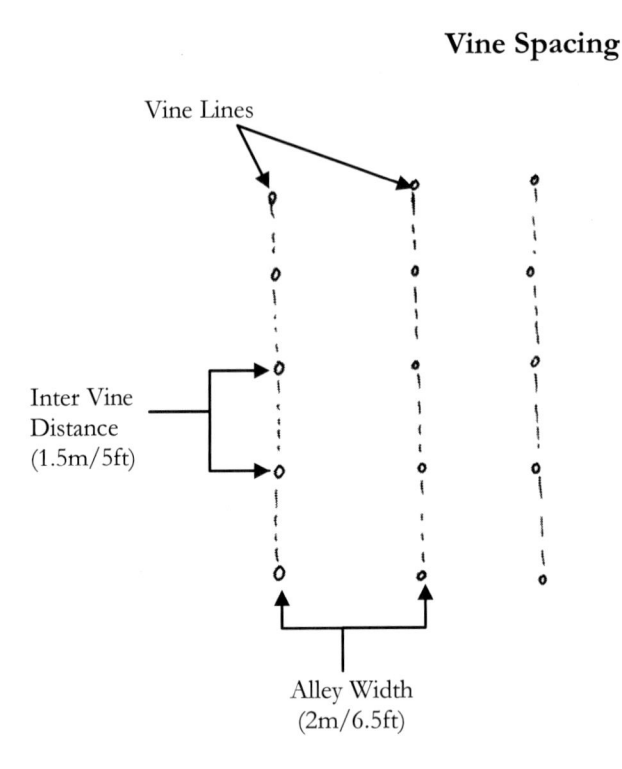

Vine Spacing

Vine Lines

Inter Vine Distance (1.5m/5ft)

Alley Width (2m/6.5ft)

With good fertile soil, each vine should grow well and produce a lot of foliage. In fact chances are they will grow so well you'll have to be quite harsh when it comes to summer canopy management (see Chapter 11). What you don't want to do is plant your vines too close together so they overly compete with each other, especially in their canopies, i.e. with one plant's foliage shading another's. I spoke with a number of experienced vineyard managers with regard to vine spacing and each gave me a slightly different answer for slightly different reasons. Many English vineyards plant at 1.2m (4ft) between each vine, but having consolidated all the information I had gathered, and taken into account the high fertility of my soil, I went for a nice round 1.5m (5ft) gap between each plant.

Looking back with hindsight, I may have been able to shorten this distance slightly to 1.4m or even 1.3m between each vine, but probably no closer given what I now know of the vigorous annual growth produced by my vines. At least employing a 1.5m gap, during planting I could lay down my tape measure and easily locate (without any mental maths) where I was going to plant my vines, with nine vines per row, spaced at 0m, 1.5m, 3m, 4.5m, 6m, 7.5m, 9m, 10.5m and 12m (apologies to those wanting imperial measurements but I'm sure you can work out the conversion for yourself). I considered fitting in one more vine along each line in my provisional designs, but I had to keep the access path clear at the front of my plot, as well as the area at the back for my compost bins and a proposed storage shed. Indeed the plans for my shed were so grand that for two of the lines I decided I would plant the last vine at the 10.5m mark (giving a line of just eight vines). Don't forget that you will need at least 0.5m - 1m (around 3ft) at the end of each line for securing the trellis system (much more on this in Chapter 9, but something you still have to consider in detail even at this early planning stage).

Distance Between the Rows

As to the distance between vine rows (the width of your *alleys*), this is something again you need to consider very carefully long before you plant your vines. The distance between the rows dictates not just how close the individual vines are to each other in the second linear dimension (perpendicular to their proximity along each vine line), but also how much the foliage of one line will shade the canopy (and fruit) of the next line along as the sun moves through the sky. There is also a third reason why the distance between the vine lines is so important to get right - between the rows of vines on an urban allotment vineyard you can do something quite special and that is to grow more stuff. I'll return to this in much more detail in Chapter 6.

In commercial vineyards, the space between the rows is generally mowed grass or bare soil and the alley width is usually dictated by the width of the tractor you hope to get down the rows - you need it wide enough to chug down the vineyard carrying out the assorted jobs of a commercial enterprise, from spraying and canopy management, to pruning and picking and mowing the grass. In many British vineyards the alleys can be 3m wide, able to accommodate a nice hefty New Holland tractor. Abroad, where much of the work is done by unmechanised means (and more by people), the rows are often much closer together - this way they can fit more vines into the available space.

Wide grass alleys at Bolney Wine Estate, West Sussex

Urban Vineyard Design

As I mentioned above, one of the main issues in deciding the distance between rows of vines on an urban vineyard is shadowing. You don't want to plant your rows so close to each other that the vines cast too much of a shadow over each other during the day. My plot is around 7m (23ft) wide, including room for access paths along the length of each side. Taking a punt, I looked at a possible layout with rows 2m (6.5ft) apart. This was much less than recommended by most English commercial vineyards, but then I don't have a tractor and so girth of machinery was not a consideration. 2m apart would give quite a wide clearance for shadows during the best part of the day, and so pretty much the entire height of the vines would get complete views of the sun. I had enough room for four rows spaced across the plot at the 0m, 2m, 4m, 6m marks.

With four rows, I could have planted four varietals, but I decided to stick with my three chosen types of *Phoenix*, *Orion* and *Regent*. Given that Phoenix was getting rave reviews, I decided to go for two lines of Phoenix and one each of Orion and Regent. I was still dubious as to what sort of quality red wine I would be able to make with the Regent grapes, but in hindsight, I wish now I had planted two lines of Regent, because it makes such fabulous wine.

With all the calculations made, taking into account row spacing, inter vine distance, number of rows, types of grape and rootstock, I made contact with a commercial vine supplier down in Devon who could supply small bulk orders of bare root, grafted vines. I ordered slightly more than I needed and requested 12 Orion, 12 Regent and 24 Phoenix plants, making a total of 48 vines all grafted onto the SO4 type rootstock. This would become my urban vineyard (with some left over for the back garden and a few more for family and friends). For the sake of tradition more than anything else, I also decided to plant a small (dwarf) rose bush at the end of each line. These were traditionally used in vineyards as indicators of an incoming mildew attack, as the mildew would show on the rose leaves prior to the grapevines, but I just wanted a bit of colour.

The Urban Vineyard

If you're itching to plant your vines, or planning your vineyard in a garden setting, you might want to jump ahead to Chapter 7 - you can always come back later. But if your urban vineyard is on an allotment or small plot of land, then read on to Chapter 6.

The Urban Vineyard gets a shed

6. Between the Rows

Although you need to have a physical gap between your vine lines to prevent one line's foliage from shading the next, I soon realised this space didn't need to be dead space and go unused.

Grass Alleys

If you go to any British vineyard, most have grass growing in the alleys between the rows of vines. As I said earlier, where tractor access is paramount, the space between rows has to be kept clear. Sown with grass, the alleys are generally kept mowed short, creating green lawn strips, though some vineyards let their grass grow a bit wilder,

New planting at Biddenden Vineyard, Kent

giving a natural meadow look gracing the area between the vines. The grass serves a number of purposes, not least moisture retention, but also, it helps reduce the vigour of vigorous soils. Now some vineyards (e.g. Barnsole near Canterbury) keep the soil in their alleyways bare. The theory here is that dark soil warms up more rapidly (than grass) during the day, then radiates its heat up to the vines come sundown, effectively extending the growing day - especially useful during ripening.

During the planning stages of my urban vineyard, I looked at the pros and cons of having grassed and bare soil alleys, but both options felt a considerable waste of good growing space on a small urban plot, particularly on an allotment site which of course has its origins in being set aside to grow food. This notion was combined with the fact that if my small plot of land had high fertility, a vigour which in itself may give my vines a bit too much by way of nutrients (and cause them to produce lots of leaves but not necessarily make more berries), surely there was something I could do that would help *reduce* the vigour in the soil and at the same time make good use of the growing space between the rows. With 2m (nearly 7ft) between each row, it dawned on me that there was room to do something much more useful than just growing grass or having bare mud between the rows, and that something useful was to grow fruit and veg.

Vegetables in the Vineyard?

A plan formed in my mind that with four rows of grapevines, I had three usable alleyway spaces in which I could grow some traditional allotment fare like beans, leeks and butternut squash. But I faced a dilemma of how best to use the long skinny alleyways in the most efficient and effective way - growing things between things can be tricky.

I would still need good access to both sides of each vine row. When it comes to the rigours of canopy management, winter pruning, tucking in and harvesting (see Chapters 11 - 13), having access to both sides of each vine line is paramount. Clearly I couldn't grow stuff in the alleys right up to the vines.

The first part of my plan was to install a narrow grass path down either side of each vine to allow that necessary access. A grass path is a lot cheaper than putting down gravel or bark or paving slabs, much prettier than old carpet (as is often used on allotments), and growing grass would also add to the nutrient drain to help keep the vigour of my vines at least a little in check. Grass paths also just need a mow and I had sourced a narrow width, battery powered mower which would work a treat. Note that while my vineyard did have grass paths for a number of years, later on I decided to replace them with paths made of bark on thick weed matting (see Chapter 8).

Having a grass path either side of a central open vegetable growing area posed a small problem - during the aforementioned mowing, the grass would rapidly spread into my vegetable growing area. What I wanted was some clear delineation between grass paths and vegetable zone. The solution came in the form of raised beds.

Raised Beds

The use of raised beds on allotments appears to divide opinion with regard to their potential merits. In very boggy plots, they allow you to effectively raise the level of the soil and so the roots of your plants don't get waterlogged. However, in the same vein, during dry periods, the soil in raised beds can rapidly lose its moisture and completely dry out, so they need careful monitoring during the summer months - the raised bed giveth and yet taketh away. Looking at the proposed design of my urban vineyard, if I took a cross section across its width, I planned to have the following: a narrow grass path (around 30cm/1ft wide), a vine row, the next grass access path, a raised bed growing vegetables (90cm/3ft wide), a grass access path and then the next vine row, repeated three times.

With the current surge in the *Grow Your Own* ethos, there's been an explosion of assorted (often expensive) kit to aid you in your new found adventure into the good life and one such expensive addition are pre-made raised beds. They come in all sizes, starting from 1m x 1m squares, all nicely finished, with bevelled edges and colour stains and neat fittings. But as with most projects in my life, I generally try to find a more cost effective alternative to achieve the same end goal. I initially arrived at a timber product called 'Gravel Board' - I'm not entirely sure why it's called *gravel board,* but it seemed ideal to create cheap DIY raised beds.

Cross Section Plan for my proposed Urban Vineyard

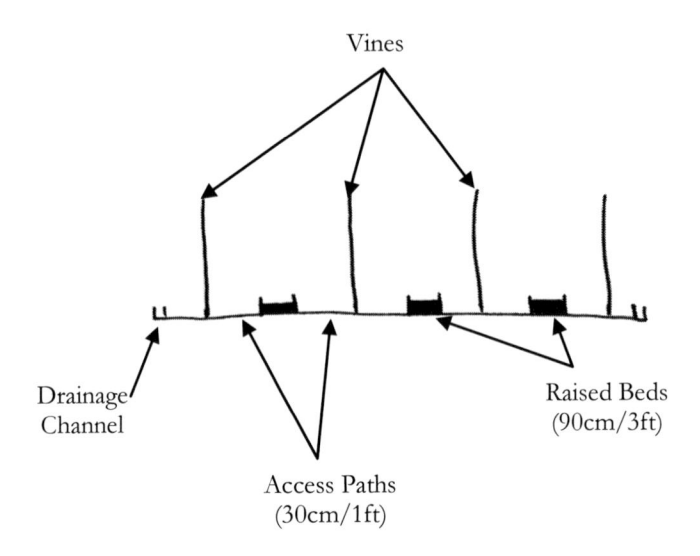

Vines

Drainage Channel

Raised Beds (90cm/3ft)

Access Paths (30cm/1ft)

The gravel boards at my local builders emporium are 15cm tall (6in in old money) and 3m (10ft) long. They also come pre-treated and so have a degree of rot resistance and by 'pre-treated', I believe this is by both pressure treatment and chemicals. Now if you feel worried the anti-rot chemicals might leach out into your gorgeously organic soil, I'm sure these boards do come in untreated form, but of course such planks of wood in close contact with moist soil would be prone to rapid rotting. I took the opinion that any chemical leachate would be minimal. As it was, rot was still an issue and several years later I replaced the gravel boards with thicker scaffold planks - jump ahead to Chapter 10 before you buy gravel boards or pre-fabricated raised beds as I would now totally recommend scaffold planks.

*The proposed sites of my raised beds,
with old carpet to keep the weeds at bay*

So my plan was to create a series of longitudinally interconnected raised vegetable beds extending down the entire length of my plot, lying between (and running parallel to) four rows of vines comprising of three varietals of interspecific hybrids (three lines of white and one of red) all planted in a North - South orientation. The plan had been made, designs had been drawn, yet after all this thinking and scheming, I still had a bare patch of muddy land.

The Urban Vineyard

My first raised bed

7. Planting Your Urban Vineyard

While I spent the winter preparing the land and thinking through vineyard designs, I had also placed an order for my vines with a specialist vine nursery down in Devon, ready for delivery the following April. The owner was good at answering all my inane and repetitive questions as I checked and double checked I had chosen suitable grape varietals. I even sent him the soil analysis report in case there was a better rootstock etc, but he assured me I had chosen the correct rootstock and had chosen my varietals well. My confidence grew as I saw in my father-in-law's gardening magazine (or possibly even my mother-in-law's copy of the *Lady* magazine) a report where a stately garden somewhere in England had chosen the very same three grape varietals as me to start their own small vineyard. I paid the deposit for the vines and waited. The time to order your vines in bulk is Autumn time when the assorted nurseries submit their orders to Germany. However, if you miss the boat and find yourself wanting to order vines come March/April, chances are that any vineyard nursery may have enough extra vines to fulfil a small order for an allotment or garden plot. If you decide to buy from a garden centre, don't buy your individual potted vines until you are ready to plant, which happens in Spring.

Preparing the Plants

In April 2008, my vines arrived. This was a little underwhelming as I was expecting them to arrive on some sort of flatbed lorry, or at least with a metaphorical fanfare of some sort. For the bulk vine buyer, no pot is needed. My 48 vines turned up in a small bag, naked from root tip to grafted twiglet. Looking back, it's astonishing to think my vines started out so vulnerable and delicate, like newborn babes, gently swaddled in blue toilet tissue, yet packed with everything they would need to grow big and strong, their whole lives ahead of them. As far as I remember the actual vine twig grafted onto the rootstock was very short, with just two buds. The accompanying note said to unpack the vines right away, keep them cool and to plant as soon as possible.

Now something I didn't use when I planted my vines (but something I have recently come across and subsequently used when planting bare rooted plants) is a fungus root grow powder called Mycorrhizal. It's readily available (I just this minute ordered some on Amazon), and I would suggest getting the packet which comes with gel, as this makes it easier to apply to bare roots. The Mycorrhizal powder helps the young vine roots grow and increase nutrient and water absorption - more about its application when we come to planting the vines.

Preparing the Ground (Again)

I measured out the position of the rows where the vines were to be planted and staked the ground with string. It's at this point that I thoroughly prepared the soil for the imminent arrival of the baby

Planting Your Urban Vineyard

vines, something that should be done for all vines, whether planted on an allotment or in your back garden. Working along the planting line, I double dug each row. What this entails is digging down one spade depth (I believe this distance is referred to as a 'Spit' in allotment parlance) and extracting said spade's worth of soil, piling it up to one side. Then get in with a fork and turn over the soil at this lower depth. What I was trying to do here was open up the soil structure directly beneath the vines. I also purchased another load of course grit sand and dug that in along each row, again to open up the soil at the macro level. Having rooted around at the lower depth, you then replace the excavated spits' worth of soil back into the trench and give that a good forking too.

Now it's at this moment that I think I may have made a slight error. Improving the poor drainage on the site was always in the forefront of my mind and despite the installation of my DIY drainage system, I still had great concerns that my soil would be too damp and soggy for the vine roots. Just as I had planned to have raised beds to grow vegetables in the alleyways, I hatched a plan to try and raise the level of the soil into which I would be planting my vines.

When I took on my plot, as I mentioned in Chapter 3, I was told that a previous holder may have taken it upon himself to remove the top layer of soil from the whole plot - not entirely sure why you would want to do that. I discovered that much of this soil had been dumped just over a low fence at the back of my plot and whatever state it had been when it was removed, it now stood as a fine pile of rotted down, good quality soil. Yes it had the odd bus seat embedded

The Urban Vineyard

in it, but this pile of earth became a fabulous source of dirt for me to replenish and build up my plot. I would literally spend a couple of hours each weekend digging out vast piles of soil from over the back, dumping it in the wheelbarrow my father-in-law had given me (when we bought him a new one for his birthday) and then distributing said soil onto the plot.

I decided that I would use most of this soil to specifically build up the level along the length of what would become the four vine rows, creating four raised ridges. Looking back, the reason why having a raised ridge (into which I would then plant my vines) could be perceived as an error is down to watering. In the Summer months, you will have to regularly water your vines (at least while they are young and sending down their first roots). By having them growing at the zenith of a raised ridge, when I watered them, the water tended to run off down the slope of the ridge, rather than soak into the ground. This is of greater consideration in the early years, as fortunately by the third year, the roots of a healthy vine should have spread far down into the soil, that the little water you can pour in next to the trunk probably is of little consequence. More on watering the baby plants in a moment because I've jumped ahead of myself.

Over each ridge, I draped anti-weed matting which I hoped would control the growth of weeds. I was trying to economise here so rather than buying four rolls and having a metre width of matting rolled out along the length of each row, I bought two rolls and cut them in half lengthwise, which in itself was quite a tricky task. The matting (now measuring 50cm wide) was rolled out along the length of each proposed vine line and held down by a growing number of half bricks to stop it blowing away.

Planting Your Urban Vineyard

The father-in-law hard at work

A quick word of warning here drawn from a time several years into the future (of running my vineyard, not some weird sci-fi action) - when I set up the plot, I used one of the cheapest weed mattings going. In hindsight I would totally advise *against* this and buy a high quality matting, otherwise like me, you will have to replace yours after a couple of years. Keeping the area under the vines weed free is of key importance, particularly during the first few years when the vines are establishing and it is recommended to have a weed free zone extending at least 30cm (1ft) each side of a vine.

The Urban Vineyard
Planting your Vines

So it came to planting day. Planting vines is something you shouldn't really do alone, so get some help. The instructions said to unpack and unwrap the vines and soak them in a bucket of water the night before planting. The following day, the baby vines were carried to their new home. Running out the tape measure along the length of the proposed lines, 1.5m interval points were marked off as planned (see Chapter 5). Working with my father-in-law as a two man team, first we cut an aperture in the anti-weed matting (a cross worked well, rather than cutting a circular hole). Then each vine was brought forth like some sort of gift for a king, bore upon hands trembling with anticipation.

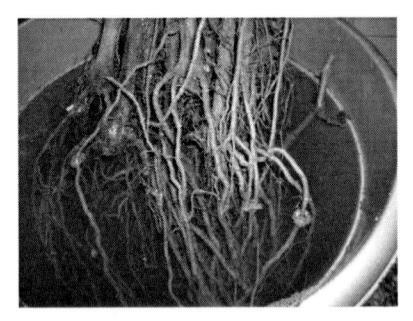

Give your baby vines a good soaking prior to planting

The instructions recommended a number of actions should be carried out as part of the planting process. First, trim the roots. This can be done using your hand as a guideline for the required root span. Place the bottom of the cane (top of the roots) at your wrist, and lay the roots so they stretch out across your hand. Then simply cut off any roots overhanging your outstretched hand. Those with small hands should probably err on the side of caution and trim to leave 10cm - 15cm (4in - 6in) of roots.

Trimming the Roots

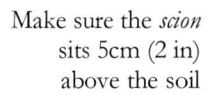

Planting Your Urban Vineyard

Next, dig a hole to such a depth that the *scion* (the bit where the actual vine twiglet is grafted to the rootstock) sits around 5cm (2in) above the level of the soil. This is to make sure only the rootstock takes root and not the base of the grafted vine via 'sucker' roots. At the bottom of the hole, place some fine sieved, quality topsoil (not compost or manure as this can burn the roots). I would suggest creating a small conical mound as then the roots can sit on it, spreading out as opposed to getting pushed flat.

If you purchased the Rootgrow Mycorrhizal fungi powder I mentioned earlier, now is the time to apply it. When you make up the solution in a bucket, the gel helps to form a thick paste. Dunk your vine roots into the paste, shake off any excess gunk, then lower the vine into your hole. A bamboo cane (or even better, one of the plastic or metal rods you can buy in garden centres) should be stood next to the naked vine. Finally, with one person holding the cane vertical, fill the soil back into the hole, again with a good helping of fresh sieved topsoil in direct contact with the roots.

Make sure the *scion* sits 5cm (2 in) above the soil

The Urban Vineyard

The tiny fledgling trunk should then be loosely tied to the support stick using paper covered twisties. During my vine growing course at Plumpton College, our tutor was insistent that the soil should not be actively filled into the hole surrounding the new vine but instead the hole should just be filled with water and you allow the water to draw in the surrounding soil, just like planting leeks. We tried this but it didn't really draw that much soil in given the size of the hole we had dug to allow the hand span width of roots a nice free stretch, so having thoroughly soaked the vine roots in water, we placed the soil in by hand. I would also recommend creating a little depression around the top of the newly planted vine to help capture a pool of water when watering.

So now I had four lovely lines of newly planted vines. The final touch was to give these still delicate plants protection from the wind and from any passing nibblers. For this I used a special plastic vine guard made by a company called Tubex. These were bought from an online supplier and came in sets of four nested together (note that Tubex do all manner of plant guards so make sure you get the Ecovine ones). These tubes also act as mini greenhouses, warming the air in direct proximity to the vines and thus help with initial establishment. I also dropped some slug pellets into each tube to protect the first bud burst from slugs and snails. My tutor at vineyard school was very insistent that you use just three pellets per tube, so that's what I did. I now had an urban vineyard.

Planting Your Urban Vineyard

The planted vineyard

The Urban Vineyard

**Aerial View of my
Urban Vineyard**

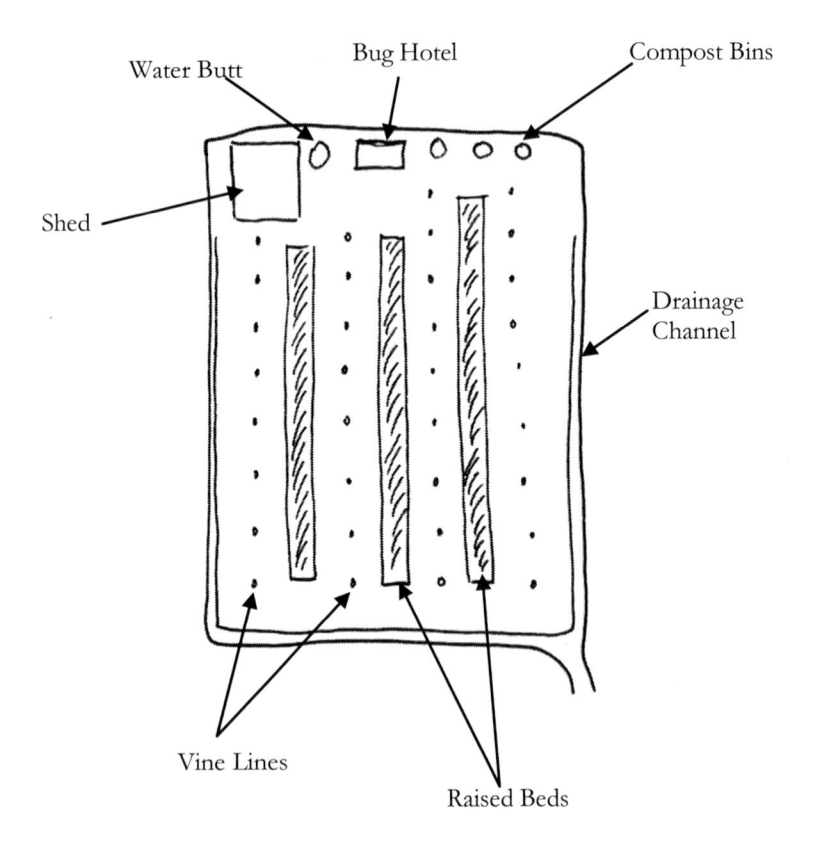

Water Butt
Bug Hotel
Compost Bins
Shed
Drainage Channel
Vine Lines
Raised Beds

8. The First Years

The first and potentially second years of the life of your vines are very different in terms of vineyard management to the rest of their lifetime and so these years warrant their own chapter. This is the time when the vines are literally finding their feet and establishing themselves and you have to give them a little extra care and attention to ensure a long and successful (and fruitful) future for your urban vineyard.

Weeds

Having planted your vines, it is imperative that along the vine rows you restrict any competition from weeds and grass. As I mentioned in

Chapter 7, I planted my vines through holes cut in weed suppressing matting and so for the general part, the matting kept any weed growth immediately around the vines to a minimum. But evil weeds like Mares Tails will push their way through and these beasts will need manually pulling out. Initially I had the weed matting extending 50cm (1.5ft) either side of the vines. However, when I came to lay my narrow grass access paths either side of each vine line, I reduced the matting width to around 25cm either side (folding half under).

Some years after I planted the vineyard, the original weed matting was looking quite sorry for itself (it was cheap you see - false economy), with all manner of weeds growing *through* and indeed *on top* of it. All it needs is a tiny bit of soil on top of the matting and weed seeds will germinate and grow. To counter this and get the vineyard weed issue back under control, I purchased much thicker, much stronger (more expensive) matting and decided to extend the matting all the way from the vine lines to the raised vegetable beds in between, effectively killing the grass. Having grass paths was fun at the beginning, but mowing them had become a bit of a chore, especially in the summer months when grass grows at a phenomenal rate. I also decided to cover my new matted access paths with chipped bark. In some respects, maybe I should have done this from the start, but you live and learn, and at the very start of my urban vineyard adventure, I liked the idea of grass pathways.

If you don't use weed matting around your vines, you could use a herbicide to keep the weeds under control, just make sure it doesn't come into contact with the baby vines. Alternatively, you could try regularly hoeing the soil directly beneath the vines and along the vine lines. This is perfectly adequate in a garden vineyard if you only have a few vines. The only problem with regular hoeing is that some vine roots can be quite shallow and lie just under the soil surface - hoeing would damage these. However there is a theory that by constantly disturbing the first couple of centimetres of soil under a vine, you encourage the vine's roots to go deep, which is a benefit.

As I mentioned earlier, placing a plastic vine guard (e.g. the Tubex Ecovine) around each baby vine acts as a mini greenhouse, warming the air and stimulating growth. However, it's just as effective in promoting the growth of weeds as the vine - turn away for too long and a huge Mares Tail will have shot up *inside* the vine guard tube. Be sure to regularly check inside each guard to make sure the leafy material sprouting up belongs to a vine and not a weed.

Watering

An important factor throughout the summer months of the first few years is water. Watering vines will become less important as time goes on, but at this stage of growth, you need to keep your young vines well watered. I found the vine guard tube to be very useful here as it not only acts as a bit of a sump (particularly if you press it into the soil a bit), but it also helps channel the water to exactly where it should go, i.e. directly under the vine. Given the sometimes waterproof nature of weed matting, if you just sprinkle water over the general vine area (particularly if you have created a raised ridge of soil like I did), much of it will just roll off and enter the ground some distance away from your increasingly thirsty vines.

Vine Growth

The aim of the first two years is to get your vines to establish (producing good root growth) and to get a healthy vine 'trunk' extending all the way up to what will become the fruiting wire. I will talk about installing and maintaining a vine trellis in detail in Chapter 9, but as with so many stages of establishing and managing your urban vineyard, you need to think ahead. You need to have some idea of what sort of trellis system you are going to use, as this will dictate what actions you take in the latter part of the first and second year (and indeed how high each vine 'trunk' will need to extend).

During the first year, initially let each vine grow as it pleases. Your vines would have come with at least two buds which, as soon as Spring arrives, will hopefully both burst into action. If your vines grow well, you might want to start encouraging them to channel their energies into growing a single strong vertical cane. By the Summer, cut back all but the sturdiest cane and let that grow. It is this cane that potentially could become the central trunk of the vine. The cane needs to be kept as straight as possible and so tie it to its bamboo support pole every 20cm using paper covered twisties. Don't use plastic sheathed wire or even worse, cable ties as these can bite into the growing cane and cause malformations. The garden twisties I use are wire ensheathed in paper, so are kinder on the stems.

As a recap, throughout the Summer of the first year, there are four basic jobs to do. Keep the weeds down, particularly those that manage to grow up within the plastic vine guards. Keep watering the vines. Keep that single shoot growing straight and after the threat of frost has gone, remove any other shoots or buds, plus any 'laterals'. The lateral shoots are the ones that come off laterally (i.e. sideways), emerging at junction points (called *nodes*) along a cane. Removing

The First Years

these side shoots prevents the vine going bushy and concentrates all its effort into growing that single strong vertical stem.

Removing laterals

In some soils, vines will grow slowly, in others (particularly old skool allotments like mine that have been fertilised for years), they can grow very rapidly. Beyond about 2m (7ft), any further growth is a waste of effort for the vines, so if they reach above your head, pinch out the growing tips. This will help the stem thicken to reach what in viticulture terms is often referred to as 'Pencil Thickness'. Basically this is a cane with a diameter around 7mm - 10mm (just under ½ inch), i.e. like a pencil - this is a hallowed measurement and something I will often refer to when it comes to further canopy management.

End of Year 1

At the end of your first year, it's time to assess the growth of each vine. It's at this point that according to their respective growths, the vines continue either onto Year 2, or can jump a year and head on to Year 3 (see Chapter 11). Leave your decision making until mid Winter, when the leaves have fallen - January is usually the best time for what will become your annual winter pruning. With each vine, assess the thickness of that single central vertical cane. If it is less than the thickness of a pencil, then grab the secateurs and calmly cut back the cane all the way down almost to the base to leave just two buds. This might seem a bit harsh (almost like you're resetting the plant back to what it looked like when you first planted it) and may feel like a waste of the first year, but beneath the surface you will have got tremendous root growth. Come the second year, the vine will grow faster and stronger.

End of Year 1

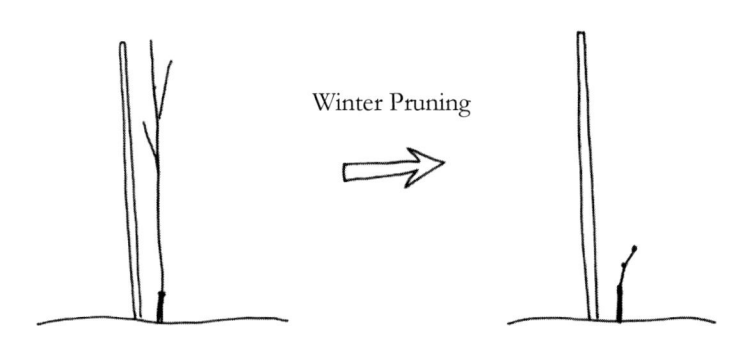

Winter Pruning ⇒

Year 2

For vines that have been cut back to just two buds, management in the second year is identical to the first year. Once again try to encourage a single cane to grow, tying it off to its support pole every 20cm or so and removing any laterals. Again if it grows above 2m (more likely in the second year), nip out the top. At the end of the second year, each vine should now have a single straight stem at least pencil thick and so will be ready to progress to the canopy management programme for Year 3.

If your vines grew really well throughout their first year and at the end of that year sport a single vertical cane thicker than a pencil, that vine can skip Year 2 and move straight onto Year 3. With a vine like this, there is no resetting back to the start. Simply cut the vine stem back down to just above the height of what will become your fruiting wire (mine is 80cm high but the height depends on what trellis you plan to use – see Chapter 9) leaving two buds. Come the new year, looking after these vines will then fall within the canopy management programme for Year 3 (Chapter 11).

End of Year 2

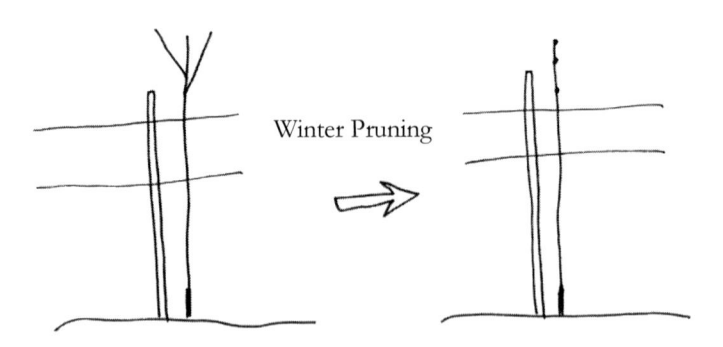

Winter Pruning

With the onset of Year 3, it's at this point in the life of your fledgling urban vineyard that you have to get going and install your support trellis.

9. Installing a Trellis

Throughout the first year or so, there is no need for a trellis or any other additional support for your vines save for the individual bamboo canes. This gives you a little while to ponder what sort of trellis you might install. Trellising systems can be quite complex, their designs drawn from passed down knowledge of the intricacies of vine growth and they are directly connected with how you manage your vines to help them produce the best grapes (something I will describe in more detail looking at Canopy Management in Chapter 11 and 12).

If you poke your nose around New World vineyards such as those of California, Australia or Argentina, they appear without fail to have an extensive trellis system in place - large solid posts at the end of each vine line, each locked to the ground through an anchor system, with support posts (wood or nowadays more likely to be metal) every couple of metres along the rows, plus kilometres of assorted wires running the length of each line. However in the Old World of France, Spain and Italy, I've often seen vines growing fairly unkempt, like low shrubs, with barely a wire or post in sight. This is known as *Goblet* style. The goblet system (if you can call it a 'system') is particularly common on rocky soils with low fertility - soil on which I find it astonishing anything can grow at all.

On the volcanic isle of Lanzarote in the Canary Islands, the vines are grown goblet style, planted in the volcanic ash amongst the lava rock. There is no trellis system as such - the local custom is to dig down through the rocky ash to reach the rich volcanic soil below, and then build a wall around each and every vine using bricks of volcanic basalt rock which acts as a wind break cum water catcher. The goblet style of growing vines appears to be more a default rather than an active choice, simply because the vines can't grow that much in soils so devoid of nutrients. Yet they still grow.

The Urban Vineyard

Typical vineyard of Lanzarote, Canary Islands

In the UK, our soil is packed full of organic material and rich in nutrients. For us, it's more a case of taming and managing what will otherwise be an explosion of vine growth and trying to get each vine to channel its energies away from producing metres and metres of shoots and leaves, and more into producing lovely grapes.

There are countless choices to be made about how to trellis your urban vineyard, whether on an allotment, in your back garden or on your patio. Once again this book does not have the scope (nor the necessary attention span) to go into a wide and detailed analysis of each and every trellising system. I'll be honest, trellising is a complex subject and I have tried to simplify it as best as possible, but this is a Chapter you might want to re-read before ordering supplies and banging in posts. Having wandered many of the vineyards of England and Wales and talked to the vineyard managers, prior to planting my urban vineyard, I managed to whittle down the various options to one system, yet the finer details of the design of this system is still dependent on how you are going to eventually manage your vines in the long term. Once again, a decision made at this point of the life of your vineyard (we're talking during Year 1 or by Year 2 at the latest) requires many future decisions to have already been thought about.

To be a successful Vigneron you don't need to be an *Oracle* or have future sight, but you do need to be able to play out any actions or decisions you make *today* far into the future, and have a strong visual idea as to where each decision will lead. By that I mean you have to have visualised your vineyard in 2, 3 or 5 years time, decided how it will look and then act to make sure said actions take you to those visions of the future. It is not as simple as A going to B going to C, but more A needs D and G to have been decided before progressing to B. I may have overcomplicated that a bit, but stay with me.

Vertical Shoot Position (VSP) Trellis

The most common trellis system in the UK is known as Vertical Shoot Position or VSP. This is a relatively simple system where the vine shoots are trained upward to create a curtain of foliage with the fruiting zone located below. Other systems can be found in the UK, such as Geneva Double Curtain or Lyre, but for the sake of your own sanity I'll stick with VSP. Within VSP, there are two slightly different canopy management systems which I will return to in more detail in Chapter 11. For the moment, all you need to know is that one is called *'Cane & Spur'*, the other *'Cordon & Spur'*. While the VSP trellis system can use both, the one I will describe in detail is based on Cane & Spur. It is known as the *Guyot* system and trains one or two fruiting canes along a main wire with several wires above to support the foliage.

Installing a VSP Trellis in the Garden

Establishing a VSP trellising system is essentially about establishing a set of horizontal support wires. If you are planting your vine(s) in a garden, the best plan of action is to plant them next to a sturdy fence (ideally south facing to catch the sun). I have six in our back garden, all bar one (which is in a pot) are planted along a fence. Plant your baby vines exactly as described in Chapter 7, with a sturdy bamboo pole to act as an individual support. Now when you reach the stage of needing to start training your vine (when it has the single, vertical, pencil thick cane), you can establish a very simple trellis along the fence. Drill holes into your fence support posts, screw in some 'vine eyes' (kind of a sturdy screw-in hook but with the hook part as a complete ring), attach thick garden wire to the eyes, pull tight and pretty much you're done.

Installing a Trellis

There are a few additional factors to consider. First off, if you are growing your vines up against a brick and mortar wall, you might be able to use the type of vine eyes that you bang straight into the mortar. I have not used these (as I have solid concrete fence posts), and they don't strike me as being the strongest support structure for something that can ultimately get quite heavy (i.e. your growing vine). Obviously screwing vine eyes into thin wooden fence panels is no good as again the eventual weight of the vine and fruit will pull them out (something my mother found out several years ago in her own garden). Inserting vine eyes into concrete posts is the best course of action, though drilling into concrete posts is something that I thought (using the correct tool) should have been easy, but it is not. Not one for the battery hand drill this, as you will need quite a bit of power to drill into a concrete post and obviously a masonry drill bit. However once inserted, the vine eyes will remain solid.

Fruiting & Foliage Wires

The other thing you need to decide for your garden trellis is the height of your 'Fruiting Wire' - this is the wire upon which you will tie down the cane (known as the 'Fruiting Cane') that bears the shoots that bears the fruit. Lots of theories and research abound about the optimal height of a fruiting wire. A low fruiting wire will benefit your fruit from residual warmth radiating up from the earth below, but put it too low and you will find stooping to cut the bunches of grapes come harvest time a bit of a pain. Also foxes do appear to love a grape and will help themselves. I would suggest having your fruiting wire at around 80cm - 100cm (2½ft) height. Simply cut a length of sturdy garden wire, insert into the vine eye, loop back and twist to secure. Same at the other end. If during the coming years you need to tighten the wire, simply untwist, pull through and re-twist to secure.

A second wire you will need is called a 'Foliage Wire', and this is used to tuck in the vertical wall of shoots growing up off your fruiting cane. I suggest installing this around 1.5m (around 5ft) high. The only other thing with your trellis wires is to make sure there is a gap (of around 10cm/4in) between the wires and the fence or wall. This should be afforded by the straight section of the vine eye screws which will keep the wire held out from the wall. Too close to a wall or fence and any movement of your grapes in the wind and they could rub, damaging the fruit.

Garden Trellis

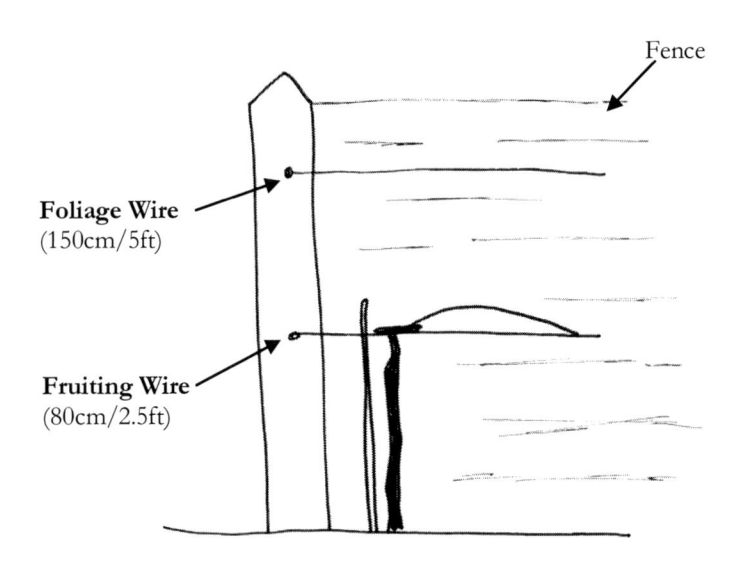

Foliage Wire
(150cm/5ft)

Fruiting Wire
(80cm/2.5ft)

Fence

Installing a VSP Trellis on Open Ground

On an allotment or other open land, you will need to install a free standing trellis - this is quite a significant undertaking. Before I proceed, let's recap what your vineyard looks like thus far. You have a number of rows of vines, with vines planted 1.2m - 1.5m (4ft - 6ft) apart along each line, with a 2m (7ft) alley between each row; each vine is tied to their own individual bamboo support cane; each vine is surrounded by a plastic vine guard. With the trellis, the first job is to install the posts.

End Posts

With posts, you have two options, metal or wood. In the past it was traditionally thick wooden posts, but now with functionality often overriding aesthetics, it's mostly metal posts that appear to grace many of our English and Welsh vineyards. The metal posts don't rot, and they already have holes drilled and places to clip-in trellis wires. All very convenient, but for me, particularly on my small scale urban vineyard, I wanted aesthetics over pure functionality, so I decided on wooden posts. I discovered that square posts (made for fencing) are very easy to come by, available from pretty much any garden centre, but what I was after was machined rounded posts which are much rarer. Whilst a square post might be fine for supporting the trellis *within* the vine lines, I wanted rounded posts at the end as they are much easier to wrap the wire round without causing undue stress in the wire.

With a huge commercial vineyard, you would need some serious sized end posts to support the trellis system, as there will be a considerable amount of weight hanging on the wires (which themselves could extend hundreds of metres). Some vineyards I've visited have end posts that look like short telegraph poles. For an allotment vineyard, your posts won't be bearing such a tremendous weight and so there's no need to get such extra thick posts for the ends. I went with machine rounded, pressure treated, pine posts 10cm diameter and 3m long (they came metric measured), already sharpened to a point, though as you will find out below, I would now recommend thicker 15cm diameter end posts.

Enlisting the help of my father-in-law, I hired a manual post basher and set about banging in the posts. The post basher is essentially a long, wrought iron cylinder with handles. You slip the very heavy device over the top of the pole, then hoist up and pull down, using its own considerable weight and your own downward thrust to drive in the post.

Installing a Trellis

Time for another quick dip into the future. Whilst most of my end posts are still fine, two actually snapped off at the base, due to rot. When it came to replacing them, I decided to go for thicker poles, around 15cm diameter. I also read up about why the original ones might have snapped at the place they snapped, i.e. at soil level, even though they were treated. It turns out it's specifically at the soil/air interface where rot can get in and attack the post. To try to counter this, I searched the web and came across a potential prophylactic solution in the form of bitumen sleeves. Prior to installing your posts, you insert the sleeve around the area where the post will sit at ground level. Then you heat the sleeve with a blowtorch to melt it into place. This is meant to give the post added protection against rot exactly where it needs it. However, in a recent conversation with a fencing installer, he commented that the usefulness of such a sheath is yet to be proved.

87

The Urban Vineyard

Anchoring the End Posts

Visit any vineyard and you will see that the end posts are generally at a 60° angle to the ground (leaning away from the vines). This gives them extra leverage strength to hold the weight on the wires. Given the spatial constraints on my allotment and the fact that each vine line was to be only 12m long, I decided to go against the norm and insert my end posts vertically. If I had inserted them at an angle, I would have had to shorten the overall length of each vine line by a considerable amount - I don't believe my trellis system has suffered unduly from having vertical end posts.

Now you need to anchor your end posts. To achieve this I purchased special cast iron screw anchors - you literally screw these into the ground, angled as you would a tent peg - see the diagram opposite. When I first set up my vineyard, to connect each post to their anchor, I took a length of wire and just wrapped it round the top of the pole, then looped it through the anchor, joined the wire to itself and tensioned (see later as to how to do this). However, given the acute angle of the wire onto my vertical posts, this always struck me as not the best way to secure my end posts. Later on in the life of the vineyard, I changed the way each end post was secured to their metal anchor, taking a turn of wire around the top, looping it through the anchor and then through a turn around the middle of the post. Apologies if this sounds like complete gibberish, just glance at the diagram opposite.

Anchoring your End Posts

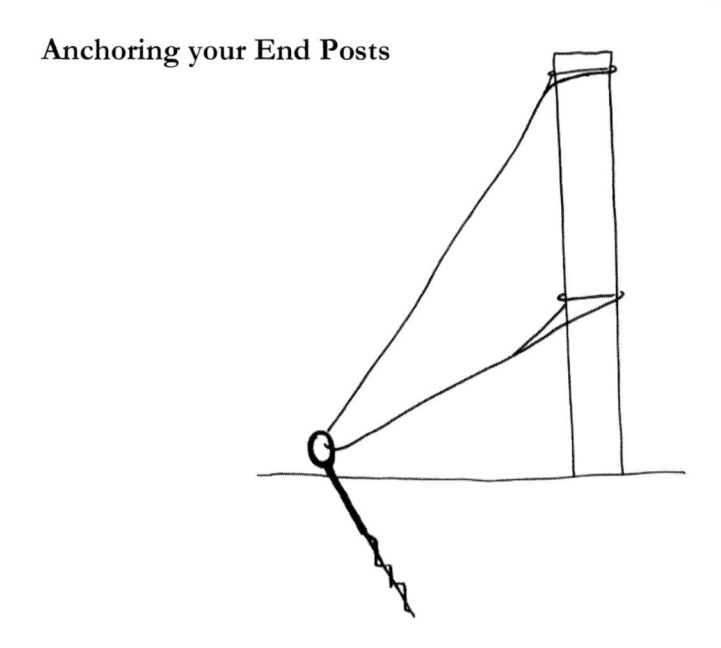

In-Line Posts

Having consulted assorted technical books on grape growing, I decided that four posts would be enough to support a vine line extending 12m long, so one post every 4m (13ft). Any further apart and you might get sagging in the trellis wires. For the posts *within* the line (as opposed to those at the ends), I would say 10cm diameter (3m tall) is fine and these can be square edged or round, but I went with round.

The Urban Vineyard

Wire & Tensioning

It's here that I need to pause to mention both the specific vineyard wire I use and the way I tighten it. For the garden vigneron, thick garden wire (available at any garden centre) works fine to support just one or two vines along a fence, with the wire secured by inserting through a vine eye and twisting back on itself. For a freestanding urban vineyard, you need to step up to industrial standards when choosing your wire. I chose a 2mm *Palais-Clos* zinc coated vine wire from a vineyard supplier called Vigo.

Now there are a few different ways to join wire together and to increase the tension in the system. One way is a simple ratchet wire tensioner in which you loop the two wire ends through each end of the tensioner, then screw it tighter. While I was doing my viticulture course at Plumpton College, I was introduced to an alternative, very neat system made by a company called *Gripple*. This system uses small, ingeniously designed metal blocks with two holes either end. There are several sized Gripple blocks for different thickness wires, so make sure you get the right one for your wire. To make a join and tension, you insert each wire into opposite ends of the Gripple block, then using their bespoke tensioning tool, you crank up the tension. It takes a little bit of getting used to and I still find it quite fiddly, especially locking the Gripple block into the tensioning tool, but soon you should get quite proficient at tensioning your wires. You can also set

Gripple Tensioning Tool

Installing a Trellis

the maximum tension strain using a dial on one of the arms of the tensioning device, so if you do get carried away, it will not over tighten. There are also blue plastic safety 'nubs' (not sure of their correct term) available from Gripple which you slip over any exposed wire ends to reduce the chance of slicing your fingers or poking yourself in the eye by sharp exposed wire ends.

Trellis Design

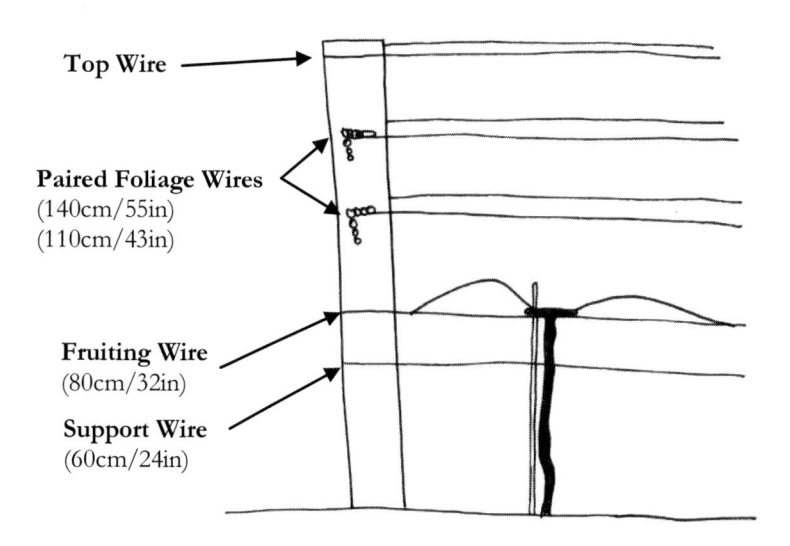

Top Wire

Paired Foliage Wires
(140cm/55in)
(110cm/43in)

Fruiting Wire
(80cm/32in)

Support Wire
(60cm/24in)

Installing the Support Wire & Fruiting Wire

With my trellis, I first installed just two wires, a lower one to support the vines (aka the *Support Wire*) located at 60cm (24in) above the ground, and an upper one which would become the *Fruiting Wire* at 80cm (32in) above the ground. Whilst this is a little low when it comes to picking the grapes (issues of bending down giving back ache), I thought it a good height to still gain some benefit from any residual heat radiating up from the earth below.

First of all, mark out the correct height on each of the posts. If you went for metal posts, this bit is a doddle as the metal posts already have holes drilled in them or have clipping-in points for the wires, so it's just a case of threading the wire through. With wooden posts, you will need to hammer in 'C' shaped spiked nails through which you then thread your wire. A word of warning - don't underestimate just how difficult it is to manage long lengths of coiled zinc galvanised wire. Now you could go the whole hog and buy a special spindle onto which you mount the wire and it unwinds brilliantly. I thought the cost of said spindle was too much, so I just fumbled with my large reel of wire and admittedly got a bit tangled up. Also, always wear thick leather gardening gloves and safety specs (even if they do make you look like *Joe 90*).

First you need to secure your wire to one of the end posts. Thread the Gripple block onto the wire's end and push it down the wire at least a metre or so. Loop the wire round the end post, then thread the end back into the Gripple. A second word of warning. Over the years, you will have to periodically tighten these wires as they become slack. If you put the Gripple joining block too close to the end post, sooner or later you will find it impossible to tighten any further and then have the difficult job of trying to un-clench the Gripple block (releasing its grip on the wires) to reposition - there is an access hole to do this, but it's tricky to operate. Take it from me and make sure you keep the

Installing a Trellis

joining Gripple block at least 30cm - 50cm (20in) from the end post as it will save you frustrating times ahead.

After securing the wire around the end post, walk the wire (without it kinking or getting tangled or even tripping you up) to the other end post and secure in the same way. Then, as best you can (a spirit level helps), secure your wire in place to the posts along the vine line with C-shaped nails. If you've gone for metal posts, you simply thread the wire through the pre-drilled holes or hook it in at the appropriate height using the conveniently placed built-in hooks. The recommendation is for the wire to be secured to the 'up wind' or windward side of your posts should you have a prevailing wind side.

The role of the lower *Support Wire* is to help support the vine trunks, but don't attach the vines direct - secure the trunks to their individual bamboo canes by twisties, then secure each bamboo cane to the support wire and fruiting wire. For this I use standard issue cable ties. In the VSP system, the *Fruiting Wire* (positioned 20cm above the support wire) will be the wire around which your vines will bear their fruit. As I mentioned before, there is lots of contradictory advice as to how low or high your fruiting wire should be. Too low and in frosty areas, you could extend the risk of frost damage. Also, it will be quite uncomfortable stooping low to pick the grapes at harvest time. Plus if you are prone to visits by foxes and badgers, they may eat bunches of low hung grapes. Some viticulturists claim a low fruiting wire means the grapes get considerable benefit from the warmth radiating off the sun-heated soil. Weigh up the options and go for what you think will work best for you and your plot. As I mentioned earlier, I went for 60cm (24in) high for my *Support Wire* and 80cm (32in) high for the *Fruiting Wire*.

Foliage Wires

The *support wire* and *fruiting wire* (along with the posts to support them) are all you need to install at the end of the first year or beginning of your second year. But as soon as you need to start managing the canopy (either actual Year 3 or 'jumped ahead' Year 3 - see Chapter 11), you will also need additional wires on the trellis in the form of *Foliage Wires*. These are much looser wires that come in pairs, one on each side of the posts, that hold the canopy foliage in place and

Installing a Trellis

are designed so that you can detach them from the posts, scoop up the expansive foliage and hoist it all into a vertical position, then reattach to the stake posts. I installed two pairs of foliage wires, at 110cm (43in) and 140cm (55in) height above the ground. These wires are attached to small lengths of chain links at each end of the lines which you hook over nails on the end posts. The chain links afford you the opportunity not just to tighten or loosen the foliage wires as and when you need to, but (as mentioned above) you can also unclip them to sweep the foliage up to form a vertical curtain of green. Just the other day I realised it maybe better to have the hooks turned away from the direction of the lines, as there is less chance of the chain links popping off.

Another word of warning (apologies that these 'warnings' are coming thick and fast at the moment, but you'll thank me for them in the end). I would suggest leaving on your vine guards (the Tubex plastic tubes that have been protecting your young vines since plantation) for as long as possible, but no later than the point where you are just about to bend down your first cane to tie it off onto the fruiting wire (beginning Year 3 - see Chapter 11). Otherwise you will be unable to lift the vine guards off the plants and instead, will have to cut each one in half to remove them.

So now you have your free standing trellis in place comprising a set of posts with the end posts anchored to the ground, a lower *support wire* helping to support each vine, an upper *fruiting wire* (which is where the intended fruit will develop) and two double sets of loose *foliage wires* to hold the foliage in place. For good measure, you can also add a fifth wire running along the very top of the posts. This one should be a single wire extending down the length of the line, round the end post and back to rejoin itself in the middle. This not only extends the support given to the foliage to the very top of your posts, but it also gives the foliage a horizontal cut off point. Beyond this height, the foliage can be cut back (known as *Topping Off*) using shears

The Urban Vineyard

should it insist on growing higher, done as part of summer canopy management (all explained in more detail in Chapter 12).

10. Vegetables in the Vineyard

If you've planted your urban vineyard on a small plot of land or allotment, it's time to look at those useful growing spaces located in the alleyways between your vine lines. If your urban vineyard is in your back garden, you might want to jump ahead to the next chapter, but if your garden has additional growing space, then read on.

It was during a lesson in wine appreciation in Blackheath that I had the idea of not just growing grapes in my urban vineyard, but extending the productivity of the land to include growing vegetables. Our tutor was taking us on a virtual tour around the grape growing regions of France and happened to mentioned that many French *Garagistes* (small vineyard owners that effectively operate out of their garage) grow vegetables between the vine rows on their small vineyards. This seemed a perfect union, particularly on an allotment where a wide alley of grass between vine lines would be a waste of useful growing space. Plus also, in my mind the vineyard was still an experiment, a proof of concept if you like before I could entertain any bigger and more ambitious dreams of going supersize and having a commercial vineyard - if it all went tits up, I'd still have some runner beans to show for my efforts.

So what to grow in between your vine rows? As I understand it (and I could be wrong), there is nothing that you *can't* grow, i.e. there's nothing which would adversely affect the growth, development and fruiting prowess of your grapevines. So the decision was simple - I'd grow things I like to eat. There are many books on vegetable growing and many books on how to grow veggies on an allotment or in your garden, so I don't intend for this chapter to be an exhaustive manual, more an illustration of what I did (and still do), what worked well and what failed. As far as I can tell, the success or otherwise of my crops has had little to do with the associated

The Urban Vineyard

proximity to grapevines, but a lot more to do with luck and good/poor crop growing skills.

Constructing Raised Beds

As a I explained in Chapter 5, the proposed design of my urban vineyard meant that I had room for three long growing beds in between four rows of vines. I had decided (when designing the vineyard) that these growing beds would be raised beds extending around 90cm (3ft) wide and run the length of the vineyard, so some 12m (40ft) long. This would be my total growing area. Due to time and available manpower, the raised beds were not all installed at once, that's why I'm returning to them now as it will probably be about now (in the ongoing development of your urban vineyard) that you start actually putting them in.

Vegetables in the Vineyard

Over the course of the first three years, I slowly built more and more beds to increase the overall growing capacity. As I've already mentioned, I had decided to construct my raised beds using lengths of timber called *Gravel Boards*, each plank measuring 15cm high and 3m long. The boards were initially nailed (using zinc galvanised nails) to short lengths of treated 4cm x 2cm wood posts driven into the ground. It wasn't long before I discovered that these support posts were far too skinny for the job - a child deciding to stand on the gravel board (even when expressly asked not to) could snap the support wood. Plus using nails is just a waste of time. Very soon I changed the support posts to thicker 4cm x 4cm timber ('two-be-two' in old money), driven into the ground about 30cm (1ft) deep with the gravel boards now more securely attached to them using screws.

This setup worked well for the first couple of years, but then I discovered that gravel boards, while 'treated', were prone to rot when in direct contact with the soil. I would now suggest that gravel boards are *not* the most appropriate wood to use for creating raised beds in your urban vineyard. What you need are really thick, really heavy *Scaffold* boards. These come in 3m or 3.9m lengths, are around 5cm thick and are tremendously heavy (I can barely carry two of them single handedly). Scaffold boards, whilst I believe are not actually treated at all, are more resistant to rot (probably just down to their girth and the dense type of wood used), much stronger and altogether far more robust.

As for the short wooden 4cm x 4cm support posts I screwed the original gravel boards to, even these were prone to rot. So I tried something out which at the time of writing I am still unsure whether it's worth it or not. As I understand it (as mentioned before when discussing my rotten trellis end posts and the use of the bitumen sheaths), the main place of attack for rot on a wooden post is at the soil/air interface, i.e. the bit where the wood sits just at the soil line. So I conceived a plan to try to mitigate the potential for rot attack within my raised bed constructions. Taking a set of new short stakes, I wrapped each one in a plastic shopping bag, taping the top of the bag above what would become the soil line. The stake/bag combo was then driven into the ground. I'll have to let you know in four or five years time if this has helped but I thought it worth a punt.

Along the length of each new sturdy raised bed, I place flimsy broken-off bits of fencing slats just to act as moveable dividers. Prior to any planting, I dig over the soil just to break it up, plus make 'additions'. In the beginning it was shop-bought compost or left over compost from old tomato grow bags. Nowadays I pile on homemade compost taken direct from my on-site compost bins. Over the course of the first two years of taking on my plot, the raised beds were slowly added to the site, until by Spring of the third year, all raised beds had been installed and were in full production.

The newly re-installed raised beds built with scaffold planks, getting some extra soil from used grow bags

Potatoes

One of the very first non grape crops I tried on my urban vineyard was potatoes. We love fresh potatoes, particularly salad types. I was introduced to the concept of *First Early* and *Second Early* varieties, a kind of undesignated group of *Salad* potatoes and a group known as *Main Crop*. My father-in-law at plot 17 had never done well with potatoes, but given that we love potatoes, particularly small ones boiled for salads, I thought I would give them a go. Potatoes have two additional benefits for your vineyard. The first is that their bushy leaves help suppress weeds (though you will still get Mares Tails pushing through). The second is that the growth of the potato tubers helps to break up the subsoil, continuing the work to maintain good drainage.

Over the years we have had some bumper crops. I wait until the leaves shrivel (and guess that at this point the tubers are not going to get any bigger), then dig them up, getting around 10 potatoes per plant. One year we had a slight issue in that there was a horrendous frost in late May. The young tender shoots of the *Charlottes* and the *Second Earlies* (I think it was *Rocket*) got so badly burnt I wondered if we would get anything. We did, but much less than normal. Strangely the *First Earlies* bounced back and grew well.

Squashes

Another crop I was keen to grow on the vineyard were squashes and courgettes. Roasted butternut squash is a sheer delight and I love a fresh courgette in a pasta sauce. I was told by the father-in-law that both were easy to grow. Starting the seeds off in a mini plastic greenhouse thing we have in our garden at home, the young plants are taken over to the plot standing about 20cm (8in) tall. To give them a massive nutrient boost, I dig a hole about two spades-width diameter and pile in homemade compost dug straight from my on-site compost bins, then plant the young squash or courgette directly into this.

As I said earlier, the compost bins stand sentry on my plot like three midget Daleks. I fill them with all sorts of summer prunings and green material etc direct from the plot, but on occasion, I also add a bag of kitchen 'slops' from the house. Said slops consist of peelings, rotten fruit and any vegetable leftovers. Following information gleaned from our council's recycling website, I also add what is referred to as 'brown' material such as cardboard and occasionally old newspapers. This helps stop the green waste going slimy.

Vegetables in the Vineyard

Now there appear to be two schools of thought as to the best water catchment design for growing squashes. The ever knowledgeable father-in-law suggested I make a hillock (built mostly from the added in compost) into which I plant the squash and surround said hillock with a moat-like ditch. It's into this ditch that the water collects. I did this for the first season but always found the soil that made up the hillock into which the squash (or indeed courgette or cucumber) had been planted would dry out completely. Then I noticed that in most of the kitchen gardens we saw at assorted National Trust house visits, the gardeners had opted for a different design. This consists of a sunken circle, into the middle of which you plant the squash. This seemed more logical to me as I could pour far more water into this sunken sump with each watering and felt more confident I had given an effective dousing. I leave it to you to experiment.

Although the squashes have generally grown very well on the plot, there's still something I'm missing, as my output is nothing compared to the quantity and shape and colour of those borne by my father-in-law. Mine definitely look and taste like squashes, but his grow to look like the glossy photos you see in gardening books. I can only assume it may be an issue with shading from the vines? One thing I would add is to get yourself some straw and when the baby squashes appear, place a good handful under the growing gourds. This helps protect the squashes from rotting should heavy rain soak the area.

Another squash related success on our urban vineyard plot are *patty pans*. These are small, yellow squat looking courgette type things which grow in a neat clump unlike the Butternuts that trail all over the place. The trick with

103

these is not to leave them too long and instead harvest them when small, otherwise they can get a bit fibrous. Cook and eat like courgettes. Courgettes on the other hand are something that have been a bit hit and miss on the vineyard and my plants often appear to suffer a mildew halfway through the season which then creates a rather sickly looking plant that does not bear much fruit. Another issue with courgettes is water. If you are not consistent with your watering regime, then the fruit can get quite stunted and be susceptible to end rot.

Beans

By the second year, I had constructed more raised beds and with increased growing space, I decided to branch out (oh how I laughed writing that one). Obvious urban plot fare are runner beans and french beans. I grow these employing the age old triangular support system, made by lashing together a set of tall, angled bamboo canes with a crossbar running along the top. Beans are started from seed in my mini greenhouse, then transplanted across when around 25cm (10in) tall. Growth has always been good, but black fly are a perennial menace, particularly for standard issue runner beans. To try to help control these pests, I installed a Ladybird Hotel at the end of the vineyard, as ladybirds are meant to be voracious predators for aphids. I say *hotel*, it's actually more a bedsit cum condo - effectively a hollowed out lump of wood, refilled with tubes of bamboo. I believe the ladybirds are meant to overwinter there, ready to burst forth come Spring and devour all black flies. We often see them feasting on the pest aphids, but I fear most years, there are simply too many aphids and not enough ladybirds.

In an attempt to try and mount some form of permanent defence against insect attack, we also looked into complimentary planting and the construction of a bug hotel - see later.

Vegetables in the Vineyard

Staying away from using sprays, the other thing that my sons and I resort to is simply running a finger and thumb up and down the bean stalks and crushing the aphids. A chap at work also recommended spraying the beans with soapy water. Interestingly, the aphids do not seem to have any attraction at all for *borlotti* beans. In our second year, Mrs Olding came home one day with a set of borlotti bean plants a friend had passed on. I'd never heard of this variety of bean and wasn't that bothered about growing them, but it would've been a shame to waste the plants, plus I had the space. Borlotti beans grow really well on our vineyard and the beans they yield are fantastic and super versatile in the kitchen, particularly come the chill of Autumn and Winter where a fresh bean casserole goes down a treat.

Strawberries

One fruit I have always loved are strawberries. Even before I had completed the first long raised bed, I had already decided that I would have a patch of strawberries. Expensive plants were purchased online promising mammoth yields and on receipt, were then planted through holes in a sheet of weed-suppressing matting following the guidance of assorted gardening books. My strawberry plot has since been added to, using plants grown from the runners of those first pioneer plants. Choosing a few of the healthiest looking runners (ones that have already attached to the ground via little 'rootlets'), I transfer the babies into pots, grow them up and then plant them alongside their parents.

My strawberry yield has been good, but not great. I'm unsure why this is the case, and I also discovered that strawberry plants have quite a short productive life, only in the region of 3 - 5 years, so you need to keep an eye out and replace older plants.

Come fruiting season, I do two things. First I cover the weed matting with straw. This acts to keep the berries off the ground and away from any potential sitting water so they don't spoil. The other thing I do is cover them in a hooped bird net tunnel. Flocks of pigeons settle on the houses that lie adjacent to the vineyard, plus we also have to contend with the famous London Parakeets dropping in.

Raspberries

My father-in-law has a very productive plot, one that he has toiled for over 30 years. He grows all sorts, but his raspberries always grow very well. As a fan of raspberries I decided in the winter of the second year that we'd have some too. Now a word of caution - just because you can get 18 plants of three different varieties for a good price does not mean that you necessarily want or indeed have room for 18 plants. I went ahead and purchased the special offer 18 plants, with the

Vegetables in the Vineyard

promise that each variety produced fruit at slightly different times of the year, which is great because you don't want all your raspberries coming at once - that would be too many raspberries, even for me.

To prepare for their arrival, the raised bed was thoroughly manured and the baby plants (not more than roots with a stalk bearing two buds) were planted in Autumn. I also set up a very simple support system made up of sturdy plastic poles every 1.5m (5ft) with three support wires stretched across. Now as you might have guessed, 18 plants takes up a lot of space, nearly three quarters of the entire length of one of my long raised beds. This was a bit of an oversight as I didn't really want to use up all that space with one crop. Over the next couple of years I managed to sub down the raspberries to free up a bit more space. I have also found I can grow stuff like squashes alongside them. Note that raspberry plants do have a habit of sprouting up all over the place, so you'll have to keep an eye out and pull them up if they pop up in the wrong place, such as in your grapevine lines.

Given the presence of birds, I tend to net the raspberry bushes in July. Effective netting (as I will return to with the grapevines in Chapter 13) is something I have found hard to design and even harder to install. In an ideal world with lots of cash and space, I believe the best route to success is to construct some sort of cage around your entre crop and then drape a suitable anti-bird net over the whole cage. Sadly I don't have the luxury of space or cash, so I revert to throwing a net up and over the plants and securing to the ground either side with pegs. It works, but it's very fiddly and the cheap green netting I have used in the past is a nightmare to cut and prevent from tangling.

Corn

In the third year, I introduced a new crop to the vineyard, that of corn. I did try growing it from seeds, but from all my seed pots, only two grew - not sure what was going on there. However there was a fine set of baby plants at the local garden nursery which I snapped up and planted. Following a system devised by the Native Americans, my plan was to grow the corn along with a squash or two. The idea is based on the fact that the corn grows tall and the squash grows short and the two live happily together, and it does seem to work.

Other Vegetables

Now a typical allotmenteer would also grow a host of other things on their plot, not least cabbages and lettuces, broccoli and Brussels sprouts. I had a stab at broccoli, buying the baby plants already started off, but they came to nothing. I think I had a double whammy of pigeon attack plus some sort of white fly infestation. I did employ some fine anti-fly gauze, but by then I think it was too late. As to cabbages and Brussels sprouts, I don't eat them so see no point in growing them. Lettuces, tomatoes and all other salad items we grow in abundance, but in the back garden at home which makes for easy access on a warm summer evening come dinner time. For tomatoes, we grow a mixture of varieties in grow bags located in the sun trap right outside our back door next to a couple of potted grapevines.

Other non grape plants I have tried to grow on my urban vineyard include carrots, spinach, beetroot and rhubarb, not all of which are success stories. Beetroots grow well but carrots don't seem to thrive at all and again, I'm not entirely sure why. The spinach is a bit weird in that spinach I grow at home grows as it should, producing bountiful leaves which we cut and eat and then come back time and time again. On the plot however, they seem to go from small plants straight to seed producing plants without any useful edible stage in between.

When I planted my first rhubarb plant (purchased at significant cost from a garden centre), I made the mistake of trying to 'force' it straight away by putting an upturned dustbin over it. It subsequently died! Let it grow naturally for a year, then force it in its second year. The best (and prettiest) device for forcing is a terracotta forcing pot, which comes with a handy lid so you can see how your stems are growing. When it comes to picking the thin long succulent forced stems, either gently tug at the base or bend them at the base, whichever works best. After forcing, give your rhubarb a year off to grow *au naturel* again, then force every other year. And then there are the leeks.

Rhubarb in a Forcing Pot

Leeks

It has always annoyed me that the growing season is limited to the Spring and Summer, and come Autumn, the ground just sits unproductive. But then I discovered that certain leeks could be planted in late Summer or early Autumn, slowly growing through the winter ready for harvest in early Spring. This seemed to be a great thing to grow over the Winter and a good use of the land. I grew my plants from seed and planted them out just as the books told me to. The grass-like 'leek-lets' were individually transplanted into small holes created by a dibber and then water poured in to fill the soil around the plant. They grew well (whilst there was still warmth) and then sort of went into stasis over winter. This did not surprise me, as plants need warmth to grow and so it was with baited breath I waited to see how my crop of leeks would turn out come April.

Now for two years I tried growing leeks this way and each year the leeks would grow well, but not to the thick fat stage you buy in the shops, more a kind of skinny looking set, but healthy all the same. Then just as I was considering, that despite their minimal girth, I couldn't leave them any longer to fatten up, they all rapidly went to seed. A leek plant that has gone to seed is virtually unusable in the kitchen - the heart of the plant becomes a thick, inedible stalk and the outside layers are tough and not the juiciest to eat. So it was with a gnashing of teeth that I raised this issue (of my leeks going to seed before they were ready) to the father-in-law, to which he replied that leeks go to seed as soon as the weather changes and we get a little warmth back in the sun. I sighed. If only I had known about this from the start.

The solution I found is to grow leeks much earlier, planting during the latter part of Summer (and not to plant them in Autumn) using the area of my raised beds that I had just harvested the first early potatoes from. We now pick and eat them fully grown in the Winter, or leave them to overwinter, consuming them as and when required, but ensuring all are eaten by Spring before the sun's warmth triggers them to all go to seed!

Green Manure

With regards to this notion of keeping the plot productive over the winter, I have found two areas of great success. The first is growing green manure plants. Sown at the end of the Summer harvest, plants like mustard or alfalfa grow rapidly (even in the dwindling heat of Autumn). You then shred the shoots before they get too big (and definitely before seeding) and dig them into the ground. The good thing about a plant like mustard is that it not only acts as a green manure, returning nutrients to the soil, it's also meant to act as a bit of an antiseptic for the soil, killing off any potential soil borne diseases.

Onions and Garlic

Other crops I find that grow well over winter are garlic and onions. Planting out the shop bought cloves in Autumn, as the cold weather comes in, I sometimes cover the crops in miniature poly tunnels. This appears to help, though I'm not sure whether you're meant to create a hot and sweaty humid environment, i.e. with both ends of the tunnel closed down, or to have a little bit of air flow (ends open). Come April each year, we have a fine crop of onions and garlic. Harvest them before they go to seed then dry them out, and string them up, ready to use throughout the year.

Bug Hotel

Following on from a school project, my youngest son declared that he wanted to make a large bug hotel to provide all the useful bugs a five star place to stay. Whilst my father-in-law constructed the outer shell (50cm x 50cm wooden cube frame with three shelves), we set to work filling it. Following some instructions we found online, first I cut a set of short lengths of drain pipe purchased from the local hardware store, and then crammed them full with short bamboo sticks to provide all manner of nooks and crannies for the bugs to take up residence. We also added bundles of sticks, straw and broken bits of brick to the three levels to provide a further assortment of living spaces. To keep the whole thing dry, we topped the construction with a set of old roof tiles. My son even got a photo of him standing next to his bug hotel in his local Wildlife Watch magazine.

Vegetables in the Vineyard

The proud owner of the Bug Hotel

Complimentary Planting

As well as the Bug Hotel and Ladybird Condo, another experimental practice I use to help on the vineyard is *Complimentary* or *Partner Planting*. I read somewhere that plants like French Marigolds (in full flower) placed close to aphid ravaged runner beans attracts the aphids away from the beans. As I understand it, it's the golden yellow flowers that lure the pests away, but I'm not sure how effective this specific partner planting works. All I know is the aphids our way still prefer my runner beans.

Other partner planting on the vineyard includes pots of lavender, rosemary and mint (suggested while reading the father-in-law's passed-on gardening magazines), all placed at assorted locations along each raised bed. Whilst I'm not sure exactly how these work deterring various unwanted pests, I believe knowledge of their powers dates back centuries and anyway, they're not an eyesore and add to the rich variety of the urban vineyard.

Rosemary in the Vineyard

Watering

One final element to growing vegetables in raised beds on your urban vineyard is the need for watering, particularly because raised beds can dry out during the hot summer months. Watering the plot is not a chore, it's just finding the time to do it consistently and evenly

Vegetables in the Vineyard

throughout the week that can be tricky. Yes I can pop down midweek or at the weekends to deliver a deluge or two, but crops benefit more from little and often. So what I came up with is a DIY self watering system, but I will say from the outset that I am still not sure just how effective it is.

The first ingredient is a water supply. While we have several mains-fed water troughs dotted along our allotments, there is no way I can hook up to them. They are meant for the filling of watering cans, nothing more. So first I installed a sizeable water butt next to my shed and then added guttering round the shed roof to collect rainwater and deliver to the butt for storage. Next I invested in a sort of seepage water delivery system - effectively a porous hosepipe which allows water to seep out, thus delivering water along its entire length. I have three of these pipes attached (via some standard non leaky hosepipe) to a 3-way connector. Finally I purchased a battery powered timer block that sits in between the water butt tap and the 3-way divider. This is a great bit of kit, which allows you to set the current time, the time you want the valve to open (and start the water flow), to decide how often you want it to water (e.g. every 24 hours) and for how long.

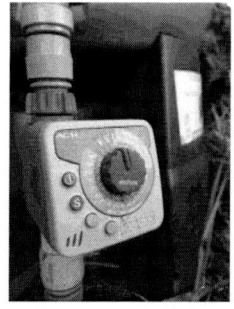

Three way connector and timer block

The Urban Vineyard

The system is perfect save for one small issue - the porous hosepipe requires a bit of water pressure for the water to squeeze out. Now if you attached this porous pipe to a mains outlet like a tap in your back garden, domestic water pressure would be fine to push the water out. Sadly my water butt, even though it's raised 30cm (1ft) or so off the ground, rarely appears to provide enough pressure to force the water out in any meaningful way. One way I try to rectify this is to mutilate the porous hose a little bit by creating small punctures in the hose walls, particularly at points where it lies alongside a growing crop such as a squash. This works fine for a couple of days, sending out a goodly stream of water. But over a day or so, I fear the holes close up. At the time of writing I have yet to fully

Vegetables in the Vineyard

solve the remaining functional issues of my self-watering system, but like I said, my urban vineyard and its assorted component parts are still very much an experiment in progress.

After such a vegetable based digression, it's time to return to the grapevines.

The Urban Vineyard

Pumpkins on the Plot

11. Year by Year Canopy Management & Annual Winter Pruning

I've already touched on many aspects of Canopy Management already, simply because of the nature of establishing a small urban vineyard means you have to know about the future, prepare for it well in advance and manage your vines as you go along. But now I'm going to break down the management activities that you'll need to do to each vine year by year for the first five years - I'll revisit Years 1 and 2, then proceed onwards into Year 3, and by Year 4 and 5, I lay out what you will be doing for the rest of the life of your vineyard (for additional season by season management practices, see Chapter 12).

Year 1

Let's just recap the early years (Chapters 7 and 8). In Year 1, the aim is to get each vine established and growing well and to provide a single, sturdy vertical trunk. You don't need a trellis or anything complicated, just a bamboo support stick for each vine, plus a protective plastic vine guard. Following bud burst, allow the plant to grow as it pleases, but then encourage each vine to grow a single vertical cane and secure this to the bamboo support stick with a paper twisty every 20cm. Just in case of late frost or rabbit attack, I wouldn't go rubbing off extra shoots until you have a good outright winning cane. If any vines choose to send out flowers, snip them off.

Over the course of Year 1, maintain that single cane growing vertically up its bamboo pole. Obviously remove any cheeky weeds that manage to grow up inside the vine guard - on my urban vineyard, Mares Tails are the bane of my life and need constant removal. If your vines show vigorous growth, and the single canes grow well, when they reach around 1.8m - 2m (around 6ft - 7ft), pinch off the growing shoot. This will then allow the cane to thicken without growing any further unnecessary height. Also take care to remove any lateral shoots. These are the shoots that come off the main cane, usually originating just above a leaf stalk.

End of Year 1 / Beginning of Year 2

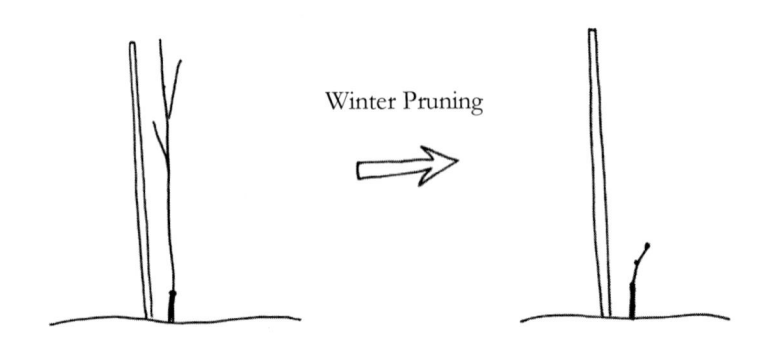

Winter Pruning

Year 2

At the end of Year 1 you have two options as to how to proceed with your canopy management depending on the state of your vine(s). Assess each vine individually as some may be more advanced (and ready to move on) than others. The first possibility is that you have a vine that has quite a short cane or a cane that has good height but very spindly. The benchmark for thickness used throughout viticulture is that of a pencil. If the cane is not as thick as a pencil, then at the end of Year 1, when it comes to winter pruning in January, you cut that cane all the way back to leave just two buds above the scion (the point where the vine is grafted to its root stock). If you don't have grafted vines, just take it down to about 25cm (10in) tall, leaving the two buds.

On my vineyard, only a couple of my vines had to undergo this brutal (but perfectly normal and necessary) treatment. For these vines, Year 2 is pretty much a repeat of Year 1. Allow a single cane to grow, making sure it is nicely vertical by tying it to its bamboo support pole (using paper covered twisties), nip out any laterals along the length of the single cane, and don't let it grow beyond 2m height - if it does, nip out the growing tip and allow the cane to thicken. Hopefully any remaining vines will achieve pencil thickness by the end of Year 2. Come winter pruning, now proceed to Year 3.

For me, possibly due to the excessive vigour of my soil, or maybe it was just a good year, but by the end of Year 1, most of my vines had a single straight cane thicker than the blessed pencil thickness standard. With these vines, you can proceed direct to Year 3.

My vineyard at end of Year 1 ready to jump on to Year 3

The Urban Vineyard
Beginning of Year 3

It's at the junction between Year 2 and Year 3 that if you haven't done so already, you will need to install your trellis (Chapter 9). No matter whether your urban vineyard is in your back garden or on an open plot of land, it's at this point you need to decide on the height you want your vines' *Fruiting Wire* and install at least that part of the trellis system (along with the lower *Support Wire*). Come the winter pruning preceding the start of Year 3 (whether this is actually your third year or if you have effectively jumped from end Year 1 straight on to Year 3), the plan for management is to set up your vine for the start of its productive life. You want to clearly establish each vine's central trunk and the point on the trunk that will become the vine's crown (the part of the plant from which all future fruiting canes emerge).

Now there are two schools of thought as to how to begin Year 3. One says you take each vine's single, pencil thick, vertical cane and bend it down to secure along the fruiting wire. The bent over cane then becomes the first *Fruiting Cane* (although whether you let it bear fruit in Year 3 is another decision - see later). A second school of thought suggests you take your vine with its single pencil thick, vertical cane, and then cut it back to leave just three buds above the position of the fruiting wire. It is from these three buds that Year 3's growth will emerge. It is this latter course of action that I took and suggest you do too.

Year by Year Canopy Management & Annual Winter Pruning

End of Year 2 / Beginning of Year 3

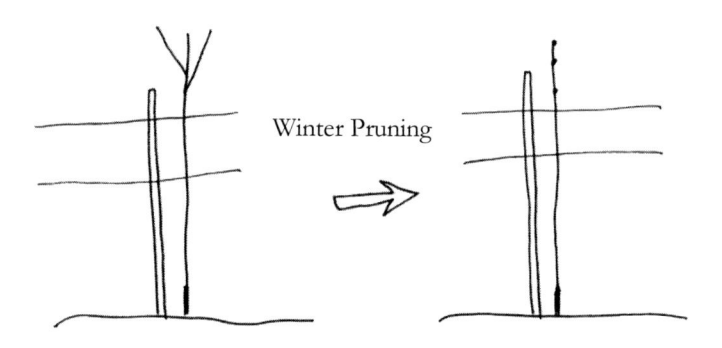

Winter Pruning

During Year 3

During Year 3, those three buds you left just above the fruiting wire will burst into action and produce canes. Allow these to grow unhindered (no need to remove laterals anymore) until they reach around 2m (7ft) height, at which point pinch them out. These three canes can now be held vertical by the addition (to your trellis system) of the loose paired *Foliage Wires* - you 'tuck in' the canes in a process called *Tucking In*, a process that will become second nature over the life of your vineyard (see Chapter 12). Any buds that pop up along the trunk part of your vines (the section extending from the ground to the fruiting wire) rub off to prevent unwanted growth. This is called, wait for it, *Bud Rubbing* (again see Chapter 12) which will be another activity you get used to doing throughout each year. Bud rubbing is a great job for a young son or daughter to start to introduce them to the joys of vineyard management. Just make sure they know to rub off only those buds on the trunk BELOW the fruiting wire. Mine seem to enjoy it and take pride in a job well done.

Over the course of Year 3, your vines will produce flowers and possibly some fruit. This can be anything from a bunch or two per vine, to quite a few bunches. This is where you have to be brave as all advice suggests not to allow your vines to produce too many berries at this early stage of their lives. Indeed, some books actually suggest a complete cull of all berries come Summertime, allowing the vines to channel all their energies into producing an ever expanding growth of roots beneath the soil, helping to initiate a long term, healthy constitution. I chose a middle ground simply due to the vigour of my plants, cutting off all small developing grape bunches, all lateral bunches, any misplaced bunches (i.e. not hanging nicely from the lower canes) and any bunches which looked a bit pathetic. It was definitely more than a Ancient Roman *decimation* (cull of 1 in every 10), but not a complete slaughter.

End of Year 3

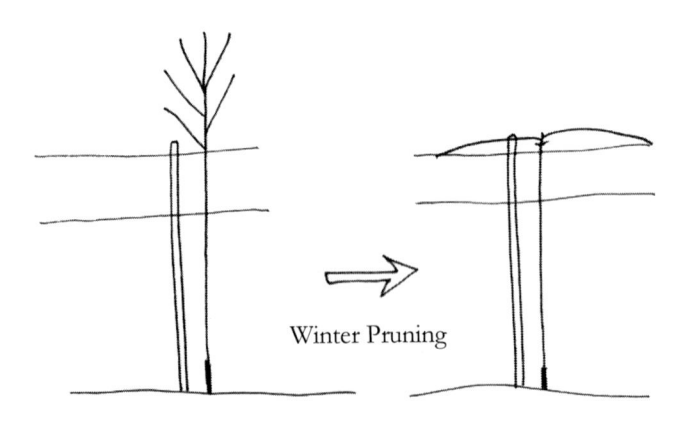

Winter Pruning

At the end of Year 3, your vines should have at least three or four healthy canes extending vertically from what will become known as the *Crown* of the vine, located just above or in line with the fruiting wire, with each cane being at least pencil thick in diameter. But now it gets a bit more complicated.

Year by Year Canopy Management & Annual Winter Pruning

Year 4

This is the moment when canopy management proper really starts in earnest, for now you have to start enforcing your chosen vine training system that will sustain your vines throughout their productive careers. We plunge once again into the *dark arts* of the ancient order of the vigneron, tapping knowledge passed down through the great Old World families and more recently tinkered with by some New World science. Before I go through what to do with your vines at the start of Year 4 and indeed onwards for the rest of their lives, let's just pause for a moment to consider what you are trying to achieve and why it's important to do it well.

There are numerous different ways to train and manage your vines, each system with its own set of pros and cons, whys and wherefores. I read about countless different training systems, from the Old World to the New World, France to Australia, Chile to USA and while I could see how one system was different to another, the chosen system sometimes appeared to be quite location specific (possibly as a result of the *terroir* or even local oenological law enforcement) or as the result of some historical influence. Oenological universities and scientific winegrowers around the world have conducted a myriad of studies into the different trellis and management systems you could use, right down to the microscopic scale, with many ongoing studies fuelling countless PhDs. If you are interested in reading further, there are now many academic papers on the subject.

For the amateur urban vigneron, I would stick to Vertical Shoot Positioning (VSP) for the trellis system which I outlined in Chapter 9 and now go into more detail in terms of canopy management. This is the most common trellis/management system in the UK and as already explained, is where vine shoots are trained upward forming a vertical curtain with the fruiting zone below. But there are some additional complications.

The Urban Vineyard
Cane & Spur vs Cordon & Spur

Within the VSP system, there are many ways to manage the canopy, but it roughly boils down to two general systems – *Cane & Spur* vs *Cordon & Spur*. I have tried to simplify where possible, and hopefully the accompanying photos and diagrams will help, but this bit of the book you may want to re-read a couple of times because its complicated stuff and you don't want to get it wrong.

Fruiting Cane (to the left) and short Spur (to the right)

The *Cane & Spur* system involves removing virtually all the canes at the end of the year and growing a whole new set the following year. In brief (and explained in more detail in the coming pages), you cut back all the year's growth to leave just one or two canes from which the following year's foliage and fruit will grow from. You also leave behind a couple of strategically placed short 'spurs'. These bear just a

126

Year by Year Canopy Management & Annual Winter Pruning

couple of buds, ready to burst into canes which are well positioned as potential replacement fruiting canes for the following year and so on. There is some evidence that the cane & spur system is more productive in cooler climates, like what we have in Britain.

An alternate system (that can still use the VSP trellis plan) is *Cordon & Spur*. In this system you establish a set of permanent, woody, horizontal extensions of the main trunk called *Cordons*. At bud burst, shoots grow out from the buds along the cordons, growing into the canes that then bear the fruit. At the end of each growing year, you cut back the canes to leave a set of short stubby spurs (bearing two buds each) spaced along the permanent woody cordons - it's then from these buds that the *following* year's canes emerge. Interestingly, the cordon management system (also used in trellis systems such as 'Geneva Double Curtain' or the 'Lyre') seemed to be the norm in many English vineyards when I first started poking around over a decade ago.

Cordon (main horizontal branch) and short Spurs

As to what system is best for you and your urban vineyard, there is no single, simple answer, and as with most decisions made about vineyards, it really depends on many factors. Most of the evidence I have read suggests that cane & spur VSP is a good system (particularly for UK vineyards) and if it's not broke, don't try to fix it (or over complicate it). All the vines in my urban vineyard are managed cane & spur on a VSP trellis, but I do have a single vine in my back garden trellised in a high cordon style for no better reason in that it allows me to practise a cordon trellis system (and indeed have photos of it for this book). I find this vine slightly less productive than the other vines, and to be honest it is a bit harder to manage during the summer.

In the UK at least, you are most likely to see cane & spur in action as part of a pruning/management system called *Double* or *Single Guyot* and this is what I now describe in some detail.

The *Guyot* System

When I was planning the design of my urban vineyard, I studied a version of Vertical Shoot Positioning (VSP) called the *Guyot* system. This was developed in the 1860s and named after Frenchman Charles Guyot. It's a fairly simple system (as vineyard trellis/management systems go) and involves the creation of one (*Single Guyot*) or two (*Double Guyot*) brand new fruiting canes each year (from which the fruit-bearing foliage will emerge) and two short spurs (from which well placed canes will emerge that can be used for the *following* year's fruiting canes). Much of the work for creating the *Guyot* system happens at Winter pruning.

Annual Winter Pruning for *Guyot*

The best time for Winter pruning is usually January or February (for the Northern Hemisphere obviously). Prune too early and the vines might not be properly asleep. Prune too late and they will have already woken up. All the leaves should have dropped and you will be left with bare canes. At the start of Year 4 you will have just 3 - 4 canes to deal with, but from Year 5 there could be quite a complex woody mess to sort out. The pruning process is effectively the same for the beginning of Year 4 as it is for the beginning of every subsequent year, so rather than say the same things twice, I have grouped the process together under the one *Winter Pruning* heading - I'm sure you will be able to follow (and I hope the photos help).

As I mentioned earlier, for the *cane & spur Double Guyot* system, you want to prune each vine to leave just two new *fruiting canes* coming from the crown (top of the trunk around the height of the fruiting wire) with one cane pointing in either direction, plus two short *spurs* (again coming from the crown) each bearing a bud or two. This process can be a rather daunting task, even for a skilled viticulturist, but particularly so for someone new to viticulture on account of the mass of foliage that grows throughout the year. Take it from me, you need to be bold and brave, as there is a lot of cutting to do, but to prune my vines to *Double Guyot*, I employ a step by step process.

The vines in January

The Urban Vineyard

A vine before Winter Pruning

First cut - remove last year's Fruiting Canes

Year by Year Canopy Management & Annual Winter Pruning

Take your pruning secateurs and advance, but be careful not to cut any of your trellis wires. At the start of Year 4, there won't be too much additional material to remove. From Year 5 onwards, there will be a mass of growth. Whichever year you are on, it's all about identifying which canes are best placed for the two different roles (next year's *fruiting canes* and next year's *spurs*).

First I remove the bulk of last year's growth by cutting last year's fruiting canes, then I cut any canes that are in the wrong position, plus any that are too spindly (less than pencil thick, particularly at the ends). After some fevered snipping, I try to leave around five or so well positioned canes for each vine. It's at this point you now need to identify the two specific canes that will become next year's *fruiting canes* and two canes that will become the *spurs*. The advice from many books is to identify the spurs first. However I disagree and suggest you first choose your fruiting canes.

Midway point - now to choose next year's Fruiting Canes

The Urban Vineyard
Next Year's Fruiting Canes

Identify two canes (one on each side) that are nicely located coming out of the crown at the height of the fruiting wire, are pencil thick, with a good set of buds. Count 8 - 10 buds along the cane moving out from the location of the crown (exclude the 'basal' bud - the one nearest the crown), then cut the cane at a point halfway between the last bud and the next one (i.e. between two *nodes*). Why 8 - 10 buds? This number is a rule of thumb, arrived at through passed down wisdom, but if you really want to get technical and are truly bent on exploring the deep, dark *magics* of viticulture, do an internet search on the word *"Charge"* pronounced as the French do with a 'sh' rather than a 'ch'. I'm not going to go into the complex concept of *Charge* suffice to say it looks at vine balance in a very rigorous, methodical and scientific way. By assessing the thicknesses of a vine's canes, the distance between buds (*inter nodal* length) and even the weight of the canes produced during the previous growing season, the process of *Charge* comes up with an optimal number of buds per vine that you should leave on each fruiting cane for next year's growth.

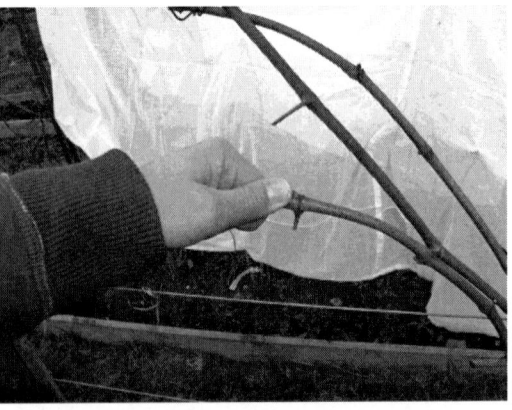

Next a tricky bit (yes, another one). You want to bend down the two canes you've chosen to be next year's fruiting canes (either side of the crown) so that they can be tied to the fruiting wire. Not just that, but you want the buds to be pointing vertically up and not sideways into the alley. This can be difficult because chances are the canes are standing erect from the crown and not extending diagonally or even horizontally along the wire. A thick cane will need a bit of help to bend and you don't want to snap it - this is why, at this point in pruning, I still have some 'back up' canes left on the vine that I haven't cut off just in case my chosen canes snap mid bend. A good tip here is to try and bend the cane between two buds (the *internodal* area). Just go slow and steady, using fingers and thumbs over the entire internodal zone (i.e. not just at one point). It will creak a bit but hopefully it won't crack or snap. As you bend it down, try to wrap the cane under the fruiting wire and tie it down using paper twisties. In some respects you want it nice and horizontal, with buds pointing straight up, making it a great platform for the forthcoming year's growth. However I found some evidence that an arched cane bowing up from the crown and then down to the fruiting wire may actually promote better berry growth. Either way, just make sure both canes (either side of the crown) are securely tied down to your fruiting wire and try not to have too much overlap of the fruiting canes from neighbouring vines.

Halfway point - new fruiting canes tied down, 'spare' canes still attached

The Urban Vineyard

Next Year's Spurs

Once you have your two new fruiting canes in place (one either side of the crown), it is now time to prepare the *spurs*. As I said above, I was advised to create the spurs first, but to be honest, I'd rather have my canes sorted before worrying about the spurs. The spurs are created by cutting canes short so they bear just one or two buds and need to be well placed to potentially become the following year's fruiting canes (see how you have to think things through with at least two years growth in mind).

There appears to be an argument as to the best position for the spurs, whether above or below the location of the vine's crown. This not only concerns the optimal position for subsequent fruiting canes, but also the optimal fertility of those future canes. My tutor at Plumpton said the spur should emerge from *under* the crown. Other books say *above*. There is a notion that (whether above or below) the spurs should be located 'nearer the roots' than the position of the new fruiting canes, so that the rising sap hits the spur first. Also the buds on the spur need to be in line with the vine line and not pointing out into the alley.

When you have identified which of the remaining canes are going to be your short spurs (one on each side), cut these canes all the way back to leave just the two buds. You can now remove any remaining left over canes from the vine (the 'worry canes' that you kept in case of snapping etc) as the job is done. But don't hang around - time to move on to the next vine.

Year by Year Canopy Management & Annual Winter Pruning

The finished *Double Guyot*

Following Winter pruning, from the beginning of Year 4 you will have a nicely pruned set of vines, each bearing two *fruiting canes* running out from the crown about 10 buds long, tied down to the fruiting wire, and one or two short stubby *spurs* coming from the crown bearing just one or two buds. You have achieved the *Double Guyot*. If you think your soil has low vigour (and consequently have planted your vines quite close together), then it might be best to go *Single Guyot*. Here each vine has a single cane and a single spur left after pruning. The spur is located on the opposite side of the fruiting cane, so that each year the new fruiting cane swaps to the other side of the crown. *Single Guyot* is also good for vines at the end of your rows or a vine located at the end of a fence. Although ideally the spur should be on the opposite side of the cane (so you swap sides each year), in this situation you will find this impractical, so the fruiting cane (and spur) stays on the same side year after year. Basically do exactly as I have described with the *Double Guyot*, but just do it all on one side.

Cordon & Spur Management

What I have just described in detail is the *cane & spur* management system for *Double Guyot*. As I've already mentioned, for the VSP trellis you can employ an alternative management system called *Cordon & Spur* whereby your vine has permanent woody *cordons* left in place each year with new canes emerging off the cordon. If you decide to

Bud on Spur

run a *cordon & spur* system, cut all this year's canes back to the two woody cordons (from which they emerged) to leave a row of spurs bearing one to two buds per spur. It's from these that the new year's fruit-bearing foliage will emerge.

Year 5 and Onwards

From Year 5 onwards, come January, you just repeat the annual Winter pruning process for each vine. One interesting note on pruning is that many books insist you don't delay, and prune your vines in the dark depths of winter (i.e. January at the latest). The reason being is if you delay, the sap might already be rising and you will get 'bleeding'. One year I was a bit delayed and come pruning, my vines were weeping all over the place. But I contacted my former

Year by Year Canopy Management & Annual Winter Pruning

tutor at Plumpton to which he replied "...Not a problem at all. It's a natural product of root pressure, and it's mostly just soil water going through the plant...back to the soil. In some ways, it's a good thing, as it will reduce the risk to the wounds becoming infected with trunk disease fungi..." So there you go.

Shhh...the vines are sleeping

Cuttings

One question you might be wondering is what to do with all those Winter prunings? Many commercial English vineyards I have visited chuck their cuttings into the vine alleys and then mow them into the ground as a neat bit of recycling. Likewise, you could always burn them. However the bulk of your pruned canes would actually make for great grapevine cuttings. Drawing on his extensive horticultural expertise, my father-in-law advised me how best to convert some of my *prunings* into *cuttings* and to make new plants - and it works. Go through all your Winter pruned canes and find all those that are pencil thick. Cut off a section just under a bud (make a straight cut). Then count up three buds and just above the third make an angled cut. These sticks (quietly bursting with nascent life) are then potted together in loose sandy top soil (not compost as this can burn new roots) and left to their own devices. Keep them well watered and come Spring they should burst into life. However you need to be a little wary as to whether a cutting has taken or not, as the emerging shoots might be driven simply by water coming up the cane, i.e. having green shoots is no indication of roots growing. What I do is let them grow in the pot (possibly 9 - 12 in a large pot) for the year, then that winter, cut them back to two buds. The following year, if the buds burst into life again, I gently lift out the cane to assess what sort of root growth has occurred. No roots and I send that cane to the bin, but if there are some roots, then I re-pot with one cutting per pot. They are then ready to grow for the year in the pot, or even to plant out.

Now there are a few caveats to mention here, the first being that, when planted out, some cuttings can still fail. Another caveat is that when I mentioned growing cuttings from my vines to a vine nursery, they suggested that such an act was actually copyright infringement (or some such) because my vines are engineered hybrids and effectively copyright protected so you can't sell them - not sure how this sits if you just give them away to friends and family. The final note came from an expert viticulture consultant who said that vines grown from cuttings can suffer trunk rot (something that grafted vines seem to have better resistance to). Whatever you decide, I know that a number of the allotments near me now have grapevines successfully growing on them made from my cuttings.

12. Additional Canopy Management Activities

Having explored the management of your vineyard year by year, I now look in detail at the activities that need to take place *within* each growing year that still fall under the umbrella of Canopy Management. The purpose of managing the canopy of your vines throughout the growing year is many fold, from ensuring an efficient leaf area surface to soak up sunlight, reducing shading and to balance the production of leaves and fruit. Ideally you want to create a uniform canopy producing (depending on varietal) around 1.5kg - 2kg (3 - 4lbs) of grapes per metre.

Goal for Annual Canopy Management

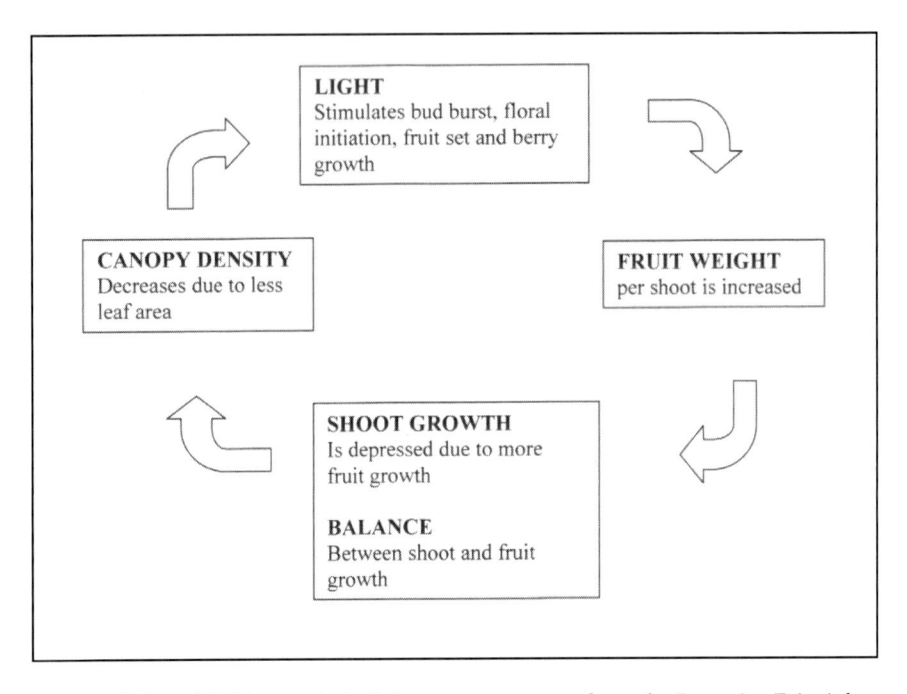

LIGHT
Stimulates bud burst, floral initiation, fruit set and berry growth

CANOPY DENSITY
Decreases due to less leaf area

FRUIT WEIGHT
per shoot is increased

SHOOT GROWTH
Is depressed due to more fruit growth

BALANCE
Between shoot and fruit growth

Source: Adapted (with permission) from course notes, from the Intensive Principles of Vine growing course, Plumpton College

Bud Rubbing

Throughout the growing season, though mostly at the start of the year in Springtime, you will need to do a bit of *Bud Rubbing*. As I mentioned in Chapter 11, you simply rub off any buds that may pop out of the main trunk below the fruiting wire (literally just rub them off with your finger tips). This stops any unnecessary growth taking energy out of the plant where it's not required. As the years go on, the number of errant buds on each vine's trunk will steadily decline, but if they do pop up, just rub them off.

Additional Canopy Management Activities

You may also have to do a bit of bud rubbing on your fruiting canes. Once you have tied down your two new fruiting canes from which the new year's growth will emerge, it is wise to see where all the buds along the cane are pointing. Some may be angled in completely the wrong direction (i.e. down) or at 90 degrees to the vine line and so a shoot emerging from there will just grow out into the alley, becoming an annoyance by getting in the way. When removing buds from fruiting canes (unlike the trunk), I would advise waiting until late Spring just in case of late frost. In 2010 we had a horrendous frost one night in May which severely burnt a number of newly emerged shoots. Fortunately I had forgotten to do any bud rubbing on the fruiting canes that year and so a number of still intact (and frost protected) buds which I had not removed came to my rescue.

Flowering

While bud burst generally happens in April/May, flowering occurs in June/July. It's during flowering that you really don't want a prolonged session of heavy rain. Grapevines are self pollinators, but downpours can upset the process of pollination and subsequent fruit setting, resulting in bunches with infertile berries which then fail to develop, something I just discovered can be referred to as 'Hen and Chickens', as you get bunches with large and small fruit. In 2012, we had such a long and protracted period of heavy rain extending right through the flowering season, that virtually all vineyards in southern Britain suffered terribly with massively reduced yields. Sadly there is basically nothing you can do about it, other than perhaps have a couple of different varietals that maybe flower at slightly different times, just to hedge your bets (or grow your grapes in a polytunnel). In my case, while the Regent and Orion produced very little fruit, the Phoenix (which must have flowered at a different time) was fine. Hailstones are also an unwanted meteorological inconvenience, but more so later on in the growing year when the berries are just plumping up. Damage by hail can split open the grapes allowing for fungal infection or for wasps to get in.

One thing I find fascinating with vines is that it takes 15 months to produce a crop. When *this* year's flowers are pollinating around June time, the *following* years flowers have already undergone a process called *Floral Initiation* and currently lie hidden within dormant buds as embryo flowers. The number of next year's flower clusters depends on the weather at this moment in time - warm weather, you get more clusters, cool you get less. So *next* year's potential crop is actually set in place *this* year.

Following flowering, from Year 4 onwards it's still a good practice to remove 'laterals' (the additional stalks that emerge out of a leaf's node), but only those within the fruiting zone. This will help reduce shading and excessive clutter come the time when the fruit is ripening.

Tucking In

Later on in the growing year, starting in the early Summer, the other thing to do is *Tucking In*. As the new shoots grow up from the two tied down fruiting canes, you simply tuck them in using the paired foliage wires. As noted in Chapter 9, this can be achieved by either physically manhandling each new shoot to sit *within* the foliage wires, or if you fancy, unhook your foliage wires and lower them to the floor, then as you raise the wires back up, sweep up all the foliage and hook the wires back in place (obviously a two person job). What tucking in does is create a tidy vertical wall of foliage which maximises the orientation of the leaves to absorb sunlight, like banks of solar panels. The best example I have seen of this, creating solid walls of leaves, is at a small family run vineyard called Barnsole near Sandwich in Kent.

Topping Off

Another activity that comes under Canopy Management mostly conducted throughout the latter half of the growing season is called *Topping Off*. I have talked about not letting your vines get too tall during the early years as this is just a waste of the plants' energy. Topping Off (also known as Hedging, Summer Pruning or Green Pruning) is the same deal, but across the whole vine line. As the growing season progresses, you simply walk down your lines and where the foliage extends beyond the uppermost wires, trim off anything that pokes above. I do this with shears but you can also go along with a hedge trimmer, just be very careful you don't cut the trellis wires.

A final part of canopy management is called *Leaf Pulling* (removing leaves around the fruiting zone) and *Cluster Thinning* (removing clusters of nascent grapes) which are both done nearer the time of the harvest. I will cover these in Chapter 13 when we look at the grapes themselves and the harvest.

Disease Control

Alongside actively managing the canopy, there are a few other vineyard activities you need to consider throughout the growing year. As I already mentioned, I don't spray my vines to counter the potential onslaught of assorted rots or mildews, but rely instead on the built-in resistance afforded by the very nature of the interspecific hybrid varietals (see Chapter 4) plus good canopy management. However it is worth just a brief note on mildews.

For non resistant varietals, there is a risk of Downy Mildew (*Peronospora*). First seen in 1878, this appears as a white velvet dusting under leaves and yellow 'oil' spots. Downy Mildew needs warm and wet weather, so not so likely in the UK. More likely is an attack by Powdery Mildew (*Oidium*) and Grey Mould (*Botrytis*).

Powdery Mildew was first identified by a Mr Tucker of Margate in 1847 and causes 'cobwebby' grey patches on leaves. Again I have found all my interspecific hybrid vines to be resistant to Powdery Mildew, but if you've planted the more classic French varietals, they may suffer and you might have to think about spraying. The concern here would be any neighbours and I would consult with them first.

Botrytis or Grey Mould infection is actually used proactively to create many types of sweet wine (like *Sauternes*). When it acts in this beneficial arena it's called Noble Rot and its 'infection' is timed to set in after the berries are fully mature, plus it's a carefully monitored process. Now although my disease resistant hybrid varietals are strongly resistant to mildews, I do find (particularly with the Phoenix) that the grapes are still susceptible to grey mould attack, particularly if there is any damage to the berries caused by wind abrasion or heavy rain which can cause the thin skinned berries to split open. The chances of infection increase substantially if I'm holding out from harvesting deep into October to get higher sugars (see Chapter 13).

If you find your vines are prone to attack, prevention is the best course of action and good canopy management goes a long way. As I

Additional Canopy Management Activities

don't spray against mildews, I'd suggest that if your vines are suffering, seek further advice on this and I would definitely try to find an organic spray. One such possible solution is the classic *Bordeaux Mixture* which is fairly widely available. There are also what are known as 'pre bunch closure botrytis sprays' that can be applied to help reduce botrytis infection.

Nutritional Deficiencies

Over the years, my vines have shown a deficiency in their uptake of magnesium. This shows up around August time by variegated discolouration in the leaves, remaining green next to the veins but then going yellow at the extremities. Magnesium is essential for the correct formation of the chlorophyll in the leaves and when I had my soil tested back at the start of this adventure, magnesium levels were high. It's possible these levels have subsequently been depleted, or for assorted reasons, my vines' ability to take up magnesium has been affected, e.g. my SO4 rootstock is noted for its poor ability for magnesium uptake (see Chapter 4). I spoke to a viticulture advisor who said that magnesium is actually a 'macro' nutrient and needed by the vines in relatively large amounts. He recommended that come Spring, you should add a dressing of magnesium fertiliser to the soil (read the instructions as to how much to add per m^2). There are a range of magnesium fertilisers available, each suited to a specific soil pH, so you will need to know the pH of your soil to know which specific fertiliser to use. An additional way to try to address this deficiency is with a foliar feed (spraying the leaves direct) during the growing season. There are all manner of foliar feeds on the market, but for the urban vigneron, I suggest using a solution of Epsom salts (magnesium sulphate) diluted 100g to 5 litres of water. I bought a neat little hand sprayer that you pump up the internal pressure and then just walk along the row holding down the trigger to deliver a fine spray. However I am unsure if my spraying regime is that effective, as in the past I have only used the foliar feed when I see the evidence of the magnesium deficiency (indicated by the discoloured leaves). My friendly viticulture advisor has suggested foliar feeding should start as soon as the first leaf is exposed and then repeated every two weeks throughout the season.

Administering a foliar feed

Additional Canopy Management Activities

A couple of other nutrient deficiencies to be aware of include lack of phosphorous, which shows up as a bluish tint on the upper surface of the leaves. Browning or reddening of the leaf edges indicates a lack of potassium. Meagre growth suggests lack of nitrogen (something I have never encountered in the urban environment) and a yellowing of the leaves (chlorosis) suggests iron deficiency. I would recommend adding a general fertiliser in Spring and perhaps after harvest, particularly to replenish potassium and phosphorus. For any more detailed thoughts on nutrition, I would recommend extending your research further, especially for best practice for alleviating the respective deficiencies.

Animal Pests

Along with birds, rabbits and foxes nicking your grapes, there are a number of other animal pests. The only one I have encountered is the *Erineum* mite, a tiny arachnid that forms galls on top of leaves with little hollows underneath. They don't seem to do a whole bag of damage, but if they bother you, you can spray with sulphur.

Evidence of mite infestation

Summary of Seasonal Canopy Management

WINTER	Pruning Trellis Repair Tying Down
SPRING	Weed control Add Fertiliser Bud rubbing Shoot removal
SUMMER	Weed Control Shoot positioning Tucking in Topping Off Foliar Feeding
AUTUMN	Leaf Pulling Crop Thinning Netting Harvest Add Fertiliser

13. The Grape Harvest

Grape berries destined to be made into wine are quite a bit different to dessert grapes you buy in the supermarkets. Generally they are much smaller, but they can also taste quite tart, even when they're fully ripe and stuffed full of sugars. The look, size and taste of the berries your vines will produce will also vary depending on the varietal you're growing. Now I grow grapevines to produce grapes to make wine. This might sound like a bit of an obvious statement, but the Turkish chaps who have an allotment near mine grow their grapevines for the vine leaves. For me, there's no point in having a lush, thick growth of vine leaves if a vine is only producing a tiny amount of grapes, or if the grapes are of poor quality. Through good canopy management, you are training your vines to direct their energies into growing top notch grapes. As harvest approaches, there are a set of additional activities you need to do out in the vineyard to gently help get those precious berries nice and ripe and full of sugars. After all, it's the sugars which turn to alcohol during fermentation.

Whilst yield is important, with grapes it should always be quality over quantity. I know of many people who have a single vine in their garden and it is literally bursting at the seams with bunches of grapes. This is fine for a nice shady arbour, occasional eating and great for birds, but not so good for making wine. Simple mechanics tells you that the more berries a single vine produces, the further the vine has to spread the sugars being formed in its solar powered leaves. In effect, an over abundance of berries can give a severe dilution of quality. I'm not saying you don't want a vast haul of grapes, but it is all about balancing quality with yield.

Balance

This term *Balance* is banded around a lot in viticulture circles. Just as the goal of the Vintner (wine maker) is to create a balanced wine (see Chapters 15 and 16), so too the goal of the Vigneron (vine grower) is to have a set of balanced vines. You want vines that don't produce too much foliage, don't over crop, don't under crop and so on. When it comes to Winter Pruning in Chapter 11, I went into detail about cutting back your two new replacement fruiting canes to around 10 buds each. The notion of leaving 10 buds is a start point. It might be that the optimum number of buds for the coming year for your vines is 6 buds per cane, or maybe they can happily run with 14. This all depends on many things, including the vine varietal itself (e.g. it might have a very large inter-node distance making for very long canes if you have too many buds) and the vigour of the vine (too much vigour usually means too much green growth and potentially not enough berry growth). This is where you just have to watch your vines each year, make notes and experiment, but experimentation within viticulture can take years, as you only get to play a single hand with each growing year. With a balanced, well managed, uniform canopy, you can hope to get around 2kg (4½lbs) of grapes per metre of vine.

The First Harvest

As I mentioned in Chapter 8, in the early years it's not advisable to overburden your vines by allowing them to produce too many grapes. In Years 1 and 2, when you are coaxing each vine to create a single strong trunk, I would say remove all berries that may pop up. In Year 3, you will start getting some bunches, but most books advise to cull all but a handful of grapes. This allows each vine to concentrate its energies into growing a vast network of roots which will ultimately prolong the life and productively of each vine. I sort of ignored this a bit. My advice is certainly reduce the volume of any grapes produced in Year 3, but as I said earlier, I did this by selectively removing bunches of grapes rather than removing everything.

Come Year 4 onwards, you are practically at full production, but now you still have to think quality over quantity. Whilst it may be fun to see just how much wine you can make by letting every berry grow and harvesting every last grape (I think I maxed out one year at 115 bottles or thereabouts from 38 vines), it might be beneficial (especially to the final quality of your wine) to cut back on some bunches and thin out the crop. A good canopy management scheme rigorously employed (as outlined in Chapters 11 and 12) should help prevent over cropping and excessive leaf production, but a bit of further tweaking here and there is to be encouraged.

Cluster Thinning

While it's great to have a truly bounteous crop, don't sacrifice quality over quantity. I must admit I've ignored this in the past to my peril. Your bunches of grapes should be evenly spaced along each vine, not crowded together, and ideally growing just within the designated fruiting zone (around the fruiting wire). Come July, have a close look at where your bunches are and taking your secateurs, thin out the crop. The recommendation is to have just two bunches per vertical fruiting shoot. Reducing your crop by thinning out will benefit you in two ways - it will help improve the quality of the grapes you leave behind, and by spacing out the bunches, it will also help reduce the chance of rot setting in, something that can happen very quickly and right just before you plan to harvest. Honestly I have checked on my grapes one weekend, planned to harvest the next and with a bit of a warm, humid week in between, rot has set in and attacked 50% of the bunches.

Leaf Pulling

Come late August or early September, the grapes start the process of ripening or *Veraison*, and it's at this time you can step in to give them a hand. One of the simplest ways is a process called *Leaf Pulling*. There's no dark magic here - all you do is pull the leaves off the plants

The Grape Harvest

within the fruiting zone where they might be covering the ripening grapes. Obviously don't go stripping your vines of their entire solar powered sugar production machinery, merely nick out the leaves that are shading your berries. This action does two things. First, it lets the berries see the sun which helps with ripening. Second, it allows air to better circulate around the berries, reducing the risk of damp-induced rots taking hold. This is important even if you have the interspecific hybrid varietals with their built-in resistance to fungal attack as these varietals can still be susceptible to bunch rot at the very end of the season.

Removal of leaves in the Fruiting Zone

Some research suggests you should start leaf pulling as early as ten days after flowering. However removing the leaves too early can expose your berries to an increased chance of sunburn which shows up as slightly crispy browned skin (a bit like Human sunburn).

Another piece of advice is don't be too shy with the leaf pulling. Really get stuck in to your fruiting zone and strip out the leaves, alive or dead, plus any stalks that are in the way, and indeed use this time to cut off any canes that are pointing in the wrong direction (i.e. out into the alleys) as they will just get in the way come harvest time. Also, it's good practice to untangle any bunches of grapes that might have got tangled around the wires or each other, so they now hang free. Plus if there's any rot in the grapes, best to cut it out now - it won't go away and will only get worse. A final word of warning is that you have now just exposed your precious crop, not just to the sun and good air flow (good things), but also to the beady eye of voracious birds.

Netting your Crop

What bird would not be tempted by lush juicy grapes? Birds are a great menace when it comes to grapes and in the southeast of England, as well as native birds, we also have flocks of bright green Parakeets. Pigeons are a particular issue and in 2010 my back garden *Orion* vine was stripped of its entire burgeoning crop one weekend while we were away. In fact just now, while I was writing that last sentence, I heard a kerfuffle outside and went out to discover six fat pigeons gorging themselves on that very same Orion vine. Flippin' pigeons!

There are several ways to keep the birds off your valuable crop. Commercial vineyards use assorted bird scaring devices, ranging from timed bangs, to assorted audio broadcasts, to birds of prey (real or kite silhouettes). The good thing about a garden or allotment is that usually there are people around at various times of the day and just having a human presence should keep the birds from swarming and eating your fruit. Another simple line of defence is to use old CDs dangling off the trellis wires. These work (allegedly) by swinging in the wind and reflecting the sunlight, causing bright flashes which

The Grape Harvest

unnerve the birds. I'm not sure how effective dangling CDs are, but many people swear by them.

A much more effective way to keep birds off your grapes, is by directly protecting your crop by covering it in netting. My word of warning here is never buy cheap bird netting. Yes it can do the job, but it is a nightmare to work with and you end up getting it tangled up or caught in the vines. I speak from experience having initially bought cheap netting, only to buy a whole new set of more expensive, much better netting the following year. Also, when using netting, try not to wear button shirts - it's notoriously easy to get snagged.

For grapevines grown in your back garden, it's fairly easy to attach a net. I simply drape the net across the vine and secure it (with those ever useful twisties) to the foliage wire at the top, and again at the bottom (under the fruit) onto the fruiting wire.

For the allotment vigneron, there are many ways you can net your grapes, but not all are easy or entirely practical (or cheap). The first is simply to cover your entire vineyard in a single net. This may sound a bit of an overkill, but it is the most effective way to protect your crop (think of the net cages you can buy for raspberries). Such large scale netting can be seen in use right across the wine growing world. On my viticulture course at Plumpton College, the whole class (20 people) was employed to unravel and extend a monster net to cover one of their entire vineyard fields - quite an expensive option requiring lots of manpower.

The Urban Vineyard

Netting the entire vineyard, Plumpton College

The second way is to net each individual vine line. Using a net at least 4m (13ft) wide, first unravel along the length of the vine then send it up one side, over the top and down the other, securing the net either to the ground or underneath the fruiting wire, making sure all low dangling grape bunches are held within the protective enclave. This works best with a well tended wall of foliage, topped off and tucked in, and with an extra pair of hands to help out. I used this method on two of my vine lines for about six years, but always found it a bit daft to net the entire wall of leaves (along with the fruit). I also feel this method restricts air circulation through the vine.

A slightly more economical way to net your vines (and retain better air movement) though significantly more fiddly, is just to net the fruiting zone where the berries are growing. What you need here are long but narrow strips of bird netting (1m/3ft width is good). Essentially you encompass the region from the lower foliage wires, all the way down to the lower support wire. Of course, you can't just hook up the net one side, send it down, under the support wire and up the other side, as all the posts and vine trunks are in the way. So you have to make a sort of two-sided parcel. Walking along the vine line, I attach a separate net to each side - the easiest way to do this, is hook it on the nails that support the foliage wires. Then using twisties, join the top of the two nets (from either side) to each other just above the first foliage wires. I would say one twisty every 20cm (8in) or so. Then join the bottoms of the two nets together under the support wire. Did I mention this was quite fiddly and time consuming, but it is both effective and cost effective. I am desperately trying to find a more efficient way to net my grapes, but at the moment, this is how I roll.

Netting just the Fruiting Zone

The Path to Harvest

With your grapes netted, you now have to play the waiting game, as during the processes of ripening, the grapes steadily build up their sugars through August, September and into October. Accumulation of sugars in your berries is down to the evaporation of water from the surface of the grapes. Evaporation draws sugars into each berry from the rest of the plant. This is a good time to start tasting your berries. Some varietals will be very 'winky' (a phrase used in the Olding household meaning very tart, in that it makes you wink when you taste them). Other varietals will taste super sweet, but you can't rely too much on taste alone. It's at this point that I choose to put the 'sniff the earth' Old World approach to one side and get all New World scientific.

For me, it always appears that much of Old World viticulture is based on instinct drawn from passed down traditions and knowledge built up over centuries. Vignerons appear to rely on simple techniques and assorted natural clues to grow and ripen their grapes. However in the New World, I get the impression they love to get out their chemistry sets for a solid bit of chemical analyses. I try to get a balance between intuition and scientific interrogation.

Sugar Levels

Sugar levels in your grapes can be measured using a few different scales. The Americans prefer something called *Brix* whereas Europeans tend to use *Oechsle*. It's a bit like feet and metres, but best not to get the scales confused. One degree Brix (1°Bx), named after German mathematician and engineer Adolf Brix, is a measure of 1 gram of sucrose in 100 grams of solution. I prefer the Oechsle scale (named after Ferninand Oechsle, a German goldsmith and inventor) as it corresponds directly to specific gravity readings, e.g. 87 degrees Oechsle (87°Oe) is the same as a specific gravity of 1.087 (see later).

The Grape Harvest

Whichever scale you use, there are two ways to measure the rising sugar levels of your grapes. The first is with a hydrometer.

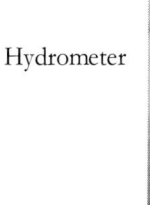

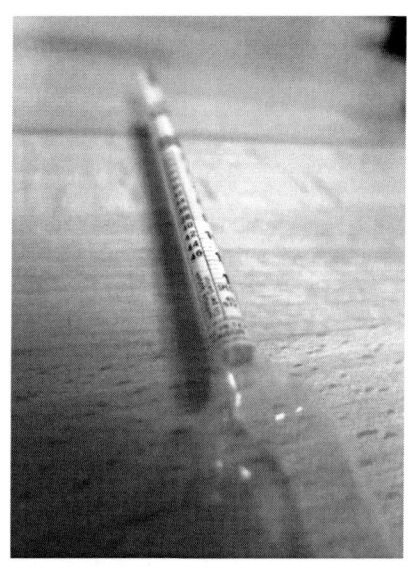

Hydrometer

The hydrometer is a mainstay of the Vintners tool kit, and something I will return to when talking about making wine in the next chapter. A hydrometer is essentially a weighted piece of glass apparatus that you plonk in a cylinder of a test liquid and then read off where the level of the liquid sits on its graduated scale. It works by Archimedes Principle and measures the specific gravity of the test liquid, which is the ratio of its own mass compared to the mass of the same volume of water. So on the Oechsle scale, 1°Oe corresponds to 1 gram of the difference between the mass of one litre of the test solution (at 20°C) and the mass of 1 litre of water (which is 1kg). You don't really need to know the mechanics of the calculation, but from a hydrometer reading, you can deduce how much sugar is in your grape juice and from that, a measure of the potential alcohol content after

The Urban Vineyard

fermentation (when all that sugar has turned to alcohol - see the table in a couple of pages time).

You will need to adjust the hydrometer reading to account for juice temperature (for which you will need an accurate thermometer) and you also have to add in a sort of 'fudge factor' which takes into account the bits of pith and seeds etc in the grape juice. As a rule of thumb and using the Oechsle (°Oe) scale, if there are bits of pulp in your sample, reduce the reading by minus 2°Oe. As for temperature, for every 5°Celsius below 20°C, subtract 1°Oe. The only problem with using a hydrometer, is you need a fair amount of grape juice to get a reading and the last thing I want to do on my small urban vineyard is use up all my grapes in the testing process.

Refractometer

A much better (though more expensive) way to assess sugar levels is to use something called a Refractometer. You should be able to get one off the internet for under £100 and with a refractometer, you only need to pick ten or so berries to get a measurement of their average sugar levels.

The refractometer works much like a prism, and relies on the fact that the density of a liquid affects its refractive index (the way it bends light). As light passes through a sample of juice, it gets bent. The amount that light rays get deflected will indicate the concentration of sugar in the juice and can be read off looking at the scale through the viewfinder. When you're done, don't forget to rinse the juice off the device.

The Grape Harvest

Refractometer

To acquire a representative test sample of each varietal's grape juice, go along each vine line and pick berries at random, roughly one or two from each vine. I say random, but I try to actively get a range of the berry sizes to represent the range of ripening grapes. The grapes should be placed in separate sandwich bags, each labelled with varietal type (don't mix them up).

Squeeze the grapes in each bag to release the juice, then pipette a few drops of the juice (minus any 'bits') onto the viewing platform of the refractometer. Close the lid (also known as a 'daylight plate'), hold the refractometer in the direction of a good natural light source, then look through. You can then read off the sugar level from the internal marker. Again the reading is almost certainly set for juice at 20°C, so you may need to dial in a slight fudge factor if your juice is warmer or cooler than this.

The Urban Vineyard

From your sugar level readings (either derived from a refractometer or hydrometer), you can read off from the table below the potential alcohol level that your wine should reach once fermentation is complete. So grape juice (or *Must* as it's called at this stage) with a specific gravity of 1.080 (80°Oe) has the potential to produce a wine with a very pleasant 10.6% alcohol level. Intriguingly, when I was researching the figures listed in the table produced below, I found it impossible to find any two tables that directly matched up, so this is my best guess.

Potential Alcohol

°Oechsle	Specific Gravity	Potential Alcohol % by volume
50	1.050	6.5
55	1.055	7.2
60	1.060	7.8
65	1.065	8.6
70	1.070	9.2
75	1.075	9.9
80	1.080	10.6
85	1.085	11.3

Source: Various

Sugar vs Acid

Come mid to late September, I take sugar readings once a week to track the progress of the ripening berries. Fast approaching is the

The Grape Harvest

most crucial and important time of year for the vine grower - when to pick your grapes? Now there's a bit of a gamble here. The longer you leave your grapes, the more sugars they should have, giving higher potential alcohol levels (unless the sun just doesn't shine in September which can happen). However, as the Autumn draws on and the air gets damper, you face a greater risk of rot setting in and reducing end yield (even with interspecific vines with their inbuilt disease resistance). Some years I have suffered significant rot on my grapes, particularly the *Phoenix* and to a lesser degree the *Orion*. While they both have resistance to mildews, Phoenix in particular doesn't have a whole bag of resistance to rots.

Alongside increasing sugars and increasing vulnerability to rot, acidity levels are also changing. Acids are what give wine much of its structure and complexity and UK wines are known for their crisp acidity (to match the crisp acid of the apples and pears we grow). Tracking the changing acid levels of your grapes is a fairly easy process and uses something called the pH scale (which is based on the concentration of hydrogen ions in solution). I mentioned this briefly in Chapter 4 when talking about assessing and adjusting the pH of your soil.

A pH less than 7 is termed 'Acid', with acid strength increasing as the pH numbers decrease. Higher pH (above 7) is 'Alkali' with strength increasing upwards to a pH of 14. A pH of 7 is Neutral. To measure the pH of your grape juice you can buy something called Universal Indicator dipsticks whose colour changes depending on the pH level - you compare the resultant colour with the chart that accompanies the sticks. I prefer to use a cheap, electronic, school-type

The Urban Vineyard

pH probe which has a digital read out. In September when I start taking readings, my grape juice is usually around pH 2.5. The recommendation is that come harvest time, grape juice destined for white wine should have a pH 3.1 - 3.4, and for red wine a pH 3.3 - 3.6. The actual acid makeup of wine (not just its overall acid level) is something I address later on in the kitchen winery (see Chapter 14).

As sugars rise, acids drop, and low acids can lead to a rather lifeless and flabby wine. Hence the gamble I mentioned above about leaving grapes on the vine for too long. I hedge my bets and try to leave the berries as long as possible, all the time taking weekly readings of the rising sugar levels and decreasing acid levels, whilst also keeping an eye on the progress of any rot. I harvest at the point I think I've reached the best of both worlds. Over the years, acid levels of my juice have always been around the pH 3.5 mark at harvest, but I have seen a range of sugar levels, with Regent peaking at 87°Oe, Phoenix at 84°Oe and Orion at 83°Oe, all in 2009, the first year I made a small harvest (my Year 3). Around 80°Oe and you are nearly at 11% alcohol by volume so these levels are pretty fair going for our climate.

My advice is not to hold on too long trying to squeeze every last sun beam into making sugars and perhaps pick a little earlier to avoid any end of season rot setting in. A friendly viticulture advisor said he picked his Phoenix at around the 70°Oe mark (due to its susceptibility to rot), then picked his Orion a week later. Interestingly, I've never reached the high sugar levels of 2009, and if I think about it, the acid levels have also crept up - I now find myself having to regularly add to the sugars and adjust acidity, particularly during the making of my white wine (all explained in detail in Chapter 15). Whilst I can't find any specific research on the matter, I have a feeling that I might be allowing my vines to over crop - too many grapes are being produced and so there is simply not enough sugars to go round. This is why it's so important to thin out the bunches and limit your crop to just two bunches of grapes per vertical fruiting shoot. Be brave and better wine will come of it.

Harvest Day

Ideally, if you have different varietals, they should come to their peak at slightly different times. Even with a small urban vineyard, harvesting grapes and then starting the process of converting the juice to wine is incredibly time consuming. To have everything coming good at the same time would be a nightmare to handle. It would be great to put an intended harvest date in the dairy months ahead, but this can lead to trouble. Sugars might not have built up as well as hoped or may have built too well, and no matter how good the Summer was, the changeable early Autumn weather might work against you.

Be careful not to cut the wires, the net or yourself

A warning note here is definitely do not harvest straight after rain - the bunches of grapes can hold a great deal of water and this will serve only to dilute those gorgeous sugars you have been building in your berries. Rain around harvest time is always going to be both annoying and troublesome. Come the first week of October 2010 and with the whole of the following week predicted to be wet, I decided to harvest my Phoenix much earlier than planned. They were barely pushing 70°Oe, but I felt that a lower alcohol wine was going to be better than no wine at all. Even at this stage, I had to leave behind a number of bunches where rot had already settled in, but it was still a healthy sized crop.

Getting ready to harvest

The Grape Harvest

Come harvest day, you need to get a number of things prepared, not least your home winery, as wine making starts on harvest day - more on that in Chapter 14. First make sure you have a good pair of grape secateurs. These are slimmer and more pointed than standard pruning secateurs and allow you to get in amongst the foliage and wires to cut out the bunches. Also, if you've netted your vines, your nets will still be in place. Definitely don't go opening or removing your nets the day before in preparation, otherwise the birds may get in. It's a bit of a drag, but you have to deal with the nets on the day of the harvest. I don't remove them entirely, I just go along the line I'm about to harvest and undo the twisty ties holding the nets together under the lower support wire, letting the nets just hang as I nip in underneath to get at the grapes.

All the grapes get placed (not flung) into clean plastic boxes or garden trugs. We'll come onto the need to sterilise all equipment during wine making, but at this stage, the collecting buckets don't need sterilising, yet I would suggest giving them a thorough wash. Any obvious rot in the grape bunches, I cut out there and then or just leave the bunches on the vine. Once you have your harvest, it's straight back home to start making the wine.

The Urban Vineyard

14. The Kitchen Winery

As a scientist by training (I have a doctorate in frog communication), when it comes to wine making, I definitely shift from a 'sniff the dirt' Old World mentality to incorporate a much more 'test tubes and chemical analyses' attitude. I believe this is the case for many amateur vintners who don't have the historical background of years working in a family winery in some tucked away village in the Loire Valley or hillsides of Bordeaux. Don't get me wrong, I would love to have the palette and nose to be able to conduct chemical analyses *au naturel* (for that is what the oral and nasal passages of an experienced wine taster are doing), but for me I need the help of a few instruments and chemical reagents to be able to produce wine successfully.

Making wine is not difficult. In fact, if you squash up some grapes and leave them in a bucket, the juice will happily turn to wine all by itself driven by the wild yeasts that naturally live on the berries. The resulting wine would be quite foul, more like vinegar, but it would be wine all the same. In many places in France, there are some Chateaux where very little is added to the grape juice and it's only the wild yeasts that are responsible for creating their amazing wine. You really don't have to do much to encourage grape juice to become wine, but in the same way you carefully manage the vines in your urban vineyard, by taking strict control of the fermentation process, you should be rewarded with a quality product. I say *should* - as with many aspects of viticulture, the creation of good quality wine from grapes relies on the vintner delving into what again I can only refer to as the *Dark Arts*. I don't claim to be any sort of grand wizard or master of these dark arts, but I know the essentials, and this knowledge has helped me create some very pleasant and very drinkable urban wine.

Inventory

There are several stages in the wine making process, but before we head off en route to that glorious transformation, it's worth having a quick look at your equipment inventory. Thus far I have covered kit used in the vineyard, such as pruning and grape cutting secateurs plus the hydrometer and refractometer. Now we head into the home winery, or as I call it, the Kitchen. I do know of some people that have a 'Winery Shed', but you will need access to water (and lots of it), plus as Winter sets in you don't want your winery to get too cold.

A sweeping overview of the essentials needed for making wine (detailed descriptions given later) include assorted size food grade buckets with lids, a suitable sized grape press (of an appropriate volume for the number of grapes you can grow), a pressing bag (to hold back the pith during pressing), an electronic thermometer can come in handy, assorted sized funnels and fermentation vessels (aka *demijohns*), bungs and airlocks and tubing for siphoning. As for chemicals and reagents, there's sodium metabisulphite tablets (aka *Campden* tablets), potassium sorbate, packets of dried cultured wine yeast, sterilising powder, fining agents and possibly an acid indicator and acid adjustment set. This might sound like a lot of kit, but without it, you may come unstuck. You don't need it all in one go, but it's best to have most of it at the outset and all of this is readily available from online home brew websites, details of which you can find in the online resources section at the back of the book.

Preparing the Must

The first stage of wine making is preparing what is referred to as the *Must* which is what you call a slurry of crushed grapes and grape juice. Having brought your buckets or trugs loaded with grapes direct from the vineyard (or harvested from your back garden), there's no time for dawdling and you should not leave the grapes sitting around. What you do next depends on whether you are making red, white or rosé still wine. This is covered in more detail in Chapters 15 and 16, but in brief, for red wine, you want to burst the grape berries and then let them ferment on their skins for a couple of days before pressing and continuing fermentation. With white wine, it's a case of rapidly crush, press, then ferment. For rosé, you crush the berries and leave on their skins for a short time, then press and ferment. One thing I don't cover is the production of sparkling wine, as I've never done it and to be honest, I feel it too tricky a beast for the urban vintner.

Sterilisation

One crucial factor in every stage of the wine making process is to sterilise any equipment that is going to come into contact with your grapes. As I mentioned in Chapter 13, I wouldn't worry about sterilising the buckets or garden trugs you use to collect the harvested grapes (other than giving them a good wash), but from now on, every bit of kit should be sterilised, from fermentation vessels, to tubing, to pipettes and syringes, funnels, buckets, even the grape press, and then later on, the bottles and corks. For this I use something called VWP sterilising powder - usually this is two teaspoons dissolved in five litres (or

1 gallon) of warm water for which I use one of my demijohns as the receptacle.

Destemming

The first stage for all wine production in the urban environment is destemming or getting the berries off their stalks. Now to be fair, you could leave your grapes on their stalks and do what is called *Whole Bunch* pressing. While this would save you a couple of hours of wrist aching destemming work, I find that my grape press doesn't cope very well with this (I have tried it). Plus the fine gauze straining bag I use within the grape press to try to reduce the pulp squidging out tends to get damaged if there are stalks involved. Aside from these technical issues, the presence of stalks during crushing and pressing can add unwanted woody or tannic flavours to the juice.

Commercial vineyards use huge automatic destemmers, and due to the onerous nature of the process, I did try to find a small mechanical destemmer on the web. With no luck, I turned to an array of wine books in search of a possible DIY design that I might ask my father-in-law to make (he is a skilled woodworker). Again no real joy. For the small scale urban vintner, I'm afraid it's down to manual destemming which is a fairly easy though time consuming activity - you simply grab each bunch and pull the grapes off.

At this stage of the proceedings, I lay out three buckets. To my left, the large plastic box holding the newly harvested bunches of grapes; in the middle, a sterilised food quality bucket into which I drop the destemmed berries; and on my right a garden trug into which I throw the discarded stems. This might sound obvious, but you need to keep things very organised and tidy, otherwise the whole process could descend into viticultural chaos (and you definitely don't want to go there).

The Kitchen Winery

As you pull the berries off their stems, if they split in the process, all the better, so long as the juice and pulp get caught in your sterilised bucket and not all down your leg. Also, keep an eye out for earwigs, leatherjackets, spiders and other creepy crawlies. It's inevitable that some will get into the bucket containing the destemmed berries, but I would try to restrict their number - I'm not sure how much they add to the taste of the wine. When you have finished destemming, bag up the stems and get your garden hose out. Rinse out the empty box that held the harvested grapes and the bucket into which you chucked the stems. The cleaner you keep everything, the less chance wasps will come nosing by. The bag of discarded stems can then go on the compost heap.

Crushing

After destemming, the next stage is crushing. While discussing my urban winery efforts with friends and family, it transpired that many thought you just chuck all the berries into a grape press. Don't! If you did that, the berries actually cushion each other and the press would be very inefficient at extracting juice. First you need to split open the berries in order to start releasing the juice (creating the *must*) and it is at this point in the process that I call upon some help and good honest child labour. You see, in my romantic vision of an ancient Bordeaux Chateau, I have this picture of the grapes being piled into a vast wooden vat and then everyone from the smallest child to the oldest grandpa jumping in to crush the grapes *a pied*. The volume of grapes I harvest would barely cover a quarter of the floor of the huge vats I've seen, but they do fill up my buckets quite nicely. The only thing is, it's hard to fit big feet into small buckets, but small eager feet work a treat. My sons have never needed much coercing into lending me their feet to crush the grapes and not long ago, I invested in some larger buckets so now the whole family can join in.

The father-in-law knee deep

The Kitchen Winery

Ideal work for small feet

The plan with crushing is to gently burst the skins of the berries, creating the *must*. When I started out making wine, I turned my grapes to must using a metal propeller type device which I inserted into a drill (like you would a drill bit). Switching on, it sliced through the berries and although fast, I would steer well clear of this gadget. Pulverising your berries is not what you want - just a little skin breaking encouragement. This is meant to be a gentle splitting of the berry skins, not some slice and dice axe murder type affair. The action of feet just stepping up and down is the time honoured way of releasing the juice and should be honoured as such, even in your back garden winery. Of course, if you only have a small bucket of grapes, you could always crush them by hand. Indeed you probably could get

The Urban Vineyard

away with not having a grape press at all - just place the crushed berries in a gauze bag and squeeze out the juice.

Harvesting in the UK is always going to be around October time, so chances are it could be quite chilly or damp. One year I harvested my crop under a menacing black rain cloud. Fortunately it didn't rain until I got the grapes home. Once harvested, you can't then put the process on hold, and preparing grapes for fermentation is not something you really want to do inside - the sticky juice just goes everywhere. With the rain now pouring down, I set up a gazebo in our back garden and settled down to destemming the berries by hand. An hour or so later and with cramp in my wrists, I had a 23 litre bucket full of berries, and with a little coercion, I got Number One son to come out and jump in to crush the grapes.

Must Preservation

Your grape berries have now been turned into *must*, a sludgy slurry of grape skins, pith, seeds and grape juice. At this point you must preserve your must (that confused my computer's grammar checker) - this will protect it from oxidation and prevent it from spoilage by any microorganisms that may have been on the skins prior to the start of fermentation. I recommend using something called Sodium Metabisulphite which comes in the handy *Campden* tablet form. Check the recommended dose, but generally I add one tablet (crushed between two spoons to form a fine powder) to each gallon (4.5 litres) of must. What happens next depends on the colour of your desired wine.

A simple way to crush a Campden Tablet

The Urban Vineyard

A delightful if messy family activity

15. Making White & Rosé Still Wine

There is a lot of overlap in the various processes employed to make red, white and rosé wine. What I've tried to do is tease apart some of the pertinent practices specific to making the three different wines, but rather than repeat myself in the next chapter, I've covered much of the shared ground here and would suggest you pop back as and when necessary when looking at the processes involved in making red wine.

You may not realise it, but white wine can be made from both white berries (yes I know they're green) and some red grape varietals - it all depends on what colour the juice is. In fact two of the traditional grape varietals used to make Champagne are the red grapes of *Pinot Noir* and *Pinot Meunier*. Making white wine from red grapes is however a bit tricky for the urban vintner as it involves getting the juice out of the berry without it contacting the red skins. But what you can also do with red grapes is make Rosé.

I discovered that many people, even those who like their wine, did not know how rosé is most commonly made. Many thought it was red and white wine mixed together (which to be honest it can be), but I would advise against this. For the urban vintner, rosé wine is made pretty much the same way as white wine (which is why I have grouped the two together) but with one small difference, in that with rosé you leave the juice slightly longer on the skins to extract some of that gorgeous pink/red colour.

The Urban Vineyard
Resting on the Skins

When you crush your grapes, the juice and skins are together and the juice is referred to as *resting on the skins*. For white wine, you usually want to minimise how long this remains that way - i.e. crush it and move quickly on to pressing. Saying that, there are countless white wines of the world where the juice is purposely left on the skins to extract both colour and flavours prior to pressing. On my part, due to the mechanics and time needed for me to crush and subsequently press a whole harvest of grapes, my whites can stay on their skins from 30 minutes to around 4 - 5 hours. Left too long and the white juice can pick up some unwanted flavours as far as the amateur urban vintner is concerned.

To make rosé wine, contact between juice and skins is a crucial stage in the process and it's this that gives the wine its pink colour. The longer you leave the juice on the skins, the darker the colour. For a beautiful pink wine, you don't need to leave it very long at all. In fact, the juice from my Regent grapes is blood red straight from the berry, so I give it only around 4 to 6 hours or so, just to allow the juice to get a good colour and for it to mop up some additional nice flavours from the skins. I certainly wouldn't leave must destined to be rosé wine longer than 12 hours on the skins, whatever the varietal, as it could get a bit tannic (sort of 'woody' tasting).

Making White and Rosé Still Wine

The Grape Press

After crushing the grapes by foot to create the must, the next physical process is pressing. Before I planted my urban vineyard, I started out making wine using other people's urban grown grapes. I was bought a small, 5 litre stainless steel press. It was a bit small even for the small volume of grapes I was dealing with at the time, and it took a flippin' long time to get through pressing the grapes. This small press was made up of an outer bucket with a nozzle that you attached a tube to, which then allowed the grape juice to drain off, and inside this bucket sat a perforated cylinder. The destemmed berries went into the inner cylinder, you wound down the screw and the juice flowed out. The little press seemed to do its job well, if slowly, but you couldn't press too many berries at once and the design was such that as the plunger descended, the bursting berries would occasionally evade all means of capture and squirt you in the eye. Because of the limited size, pressing took so long that I invariably hurried each individual press, as I had so many more berries to get through. When my own allotment sized urban vineyard started to produce fruit, I decided to go large(ish).

Traditional grape presses generally come in two forms. They have a slatted wooden cylinder or *cage* (into which you tip your grapes) sitting on a metal collecting tray on which the juice collects and flows out. Then there is either a

Ancient grape press, Lanzarote

central metal pole coming up through the middle upon which is attached a heavy metal plate, or it has some sort of cross beam construction to which the pressing plate winds down from. With the former, you bung your grapes into the cage, then place heavy boards on top, either side of the central pole, load on some wooden chocks and then start winding down the pressing plate. For a press with a cross beam, you tip your grapes in and wind down the press, but then have to unfasten the cage to extract the pressed skins. Both designs involve a fair amount of faff and I wanted something different.

Searching the internet I found a supplier of imported Italian presses. There were all sorts of designs and sizes and I picked a glorious 25 litre maple and steel construction. Now this specific press has a unique and rather neat design where the pressing plate is supported by a *movable* cross beam attached at the sides. This means that the whole pressing plate unit can be pulled aside when locked in its upper position allowing for the clean and easy insertion of grapes into the wooden cage and the subsequent removal of left over pressings.

As with all wine making items, prior to pressing, I thoroughly clean and sterilise all parts of the press, the gauze pressing bag and the collecting bucket which sits on the floor under the exit lip of press. This involves an initial wash with soap and water to remove any cobwebs, and then I liberally douse all parts with sterilising solution. After ten minutes of so, I then rinse off. This is obviously best done outside with access to a hosepipe and drain. I

My 25 litre Italian grape press with movable crossbeam

Making White and Rosé Still Wine

also thoroughly sterilise all the demijohns (and bungs) I think I will need to receive the pressed juice, filling each jar with sterilising solution and then giving the insides a good scrub with a curved brush which allows me to get into all the corners.

To press my grapes, first I wind the plate up to the top and swing it out of the way of the wood cage. Then I insert into the cage a fine gauze pressing bag and having placed a receiving bucket to catch the juice outflow, I pour into the pressing bag the trodden grape must. The pressing bag holds the must together and helps to stop the skins, seeds and larger particles of grape flesh from getting squeezed out during pressing. Before I swing the pressing unit back into place, I roll up the top of the pressing bag creating two ends and tie the top of it in a simple knot. Then it's time to wind down the press.

For must destined to be white wine, you'll be pressing either immediately after the foot powered crushing stage or at least within a few hours or so. For rosé wine, press the must after about 4 - 6 hours on the skins. As I said above, prior to pouring in the must, make sure your (sterilised) collecting bucket is ready at the outflow to catch any immediately escaping juice. In many commercial establishments, this

The Urban Vineyard

first juice is called the *free flow* juice, i.e. grape juice that comes just from crushing (not pressing) and is highly prized, used in their most expensive bottles. I believe this boils down to the idea that juice derived purely by the gentle stepping of a Virgin's foot (as opposed to the additional trauma of pressing) will go on to make the best wine. Having only limited resources, I have yet to make wine purely from free flow juice and always proceed immediately to actually pressing the grapes.

Pressing

With a grape press, the key is slow and gentle. Having poured a bucket of *must* (usually about 10 - 15 litres or 2 - 3 gallons) into the straining bag sat within the press and tied it off, spin down the pressing plate until it sits on the bag. With the more traditional grape presses bearing the central pole, you might have trouble using a straining bag, as the pole will be in the way, so you might have to go without. For these old style presses, as I mentioned earlier you place two semi circles of wood around the central pole, sitting them on top of the must and then place a couple of wooden chocks on top of that. Then you start to wind down the screw - nowhere near as easy as a cross beamed press!

With my press, I wind down the pressing plate until I meet resistance at which point I momentarily pause as grape juice now floods out. Over the course of about 45 minutes or so, I periodically wind down the plate a couple of turns at a time. A reminder here not

Making White and Rosé Still Wine

to go too fast - let the press do its thing. As the juice comes out, I would recommend transferring it from the sterilised catching bucket into a sterilised demijohn as quickly as possible, maybe even after each good press - you are less likely to kick over your stable glass demijohn as you might your precariously angled collecting bucket.

Once you feel you're really having to muscle the pressing handle around, stop and bring the plate back up to the top. At this point I open up the straining bag and give the crushed 'biscuit' of berries a good stir (just to break it all up) using a sterilised long plastic spoon I believe originally intended for the beer home brew enthusiast. Then I re-tie the straining bag, spin the plate down and give it one more squeeze. You'll find on this second press that not a great deal more juice comes out. Once you have again reached the stage where the press is not creating much juice, there's little to be gained by further squeezing. It's now a case of winding up the pressing plate, retrieving the straining bag and emptying the contents (now referred to as *Pomace*) into bin bags ready for relocation.

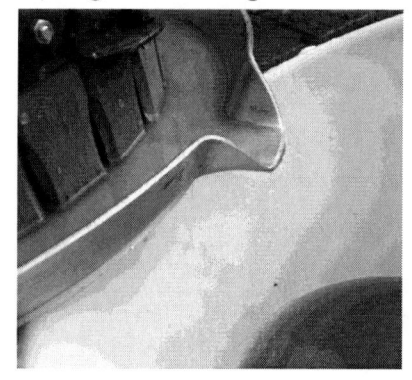

As soon as possible, deposit your bags of pomace into your compost bins. You can place it on your garden flower beds, but make sure it is far away from your back door, otherwise you might find you get infested by tiny (and very annoying) fruit flies which get into your house and pester you for months. Now it is possible to make a second beverage drink using your pomace - you add water to it, let it sit for a while, press and then ferment (or even distil which is how *Grappa* is made), but I've never taken the effort to do this.

Continue pressing the next bucket of must until all the must is pressed. With the volume of grapes I produce from my allotment urban vineyard, if I harvest a single varietal in the morning, I can still be pressing around 10pm at night. I'm afraid you just have to suck it up and get on with the job as you don't want to leave your must sitting for any longer than is necessary.

Now during the crushing/pressing processes, you have an interesting choice to make. Do you crush all your picked grapes at the same time, simply because it's a pain to keep washing and drying your feet (or your children get bored and want to do something else), or do you crush a single bucket of berries, press, then crush the next and press etc thus restricting time on the skins? I do the former and accept the fact that some of my buckets of must will have juice that has spent considerably longer on their skins (as I said, anywhere between 30 minutes to about 5 hours by the end of pressing). You may notice variations in the colour of the juice (even with white pressings) and possibly slightly different flavours in the resulting wine. This is why it's important to label your demijohns (and later, your bottles) and keep detailed notes, as these slight variations in the wine making process (quality of grapes at harvest, time on skins, specific yeast used etc) are all factors to investigate down the line when you start tasting your wines and seeing what may have the greatest influence on making the best wine.

Throughout pressing, I transfer the pressed juice from the collecting bucket into sterilised demijohns via a small funnel. Fill each demijohn then seal with a bung. It's important at this stage to make sure you fill up each demijohn almost to the top, as throughout the wine making process, you will lose a fair bit of volume and you don't want your eventual fermenting vessel to have a big air gap (reasons given later).

Leave the sealed demijohns of pressed juice for a couple of days to settle - remember you have already preserved the must with crushed Campden tablets so it should be quite safe from spoilage.

Demijohns

Just a quick note on demijohns. Demijohns (or Carboys) are what small fermentation vessels are known as. Apparently a *demijohn* is any sort of glass vessel with a wide body but small neck. When I started out making wine, it was with wine making kits purchased off the internet which provided the grape juice, chemicals, yeast and all the associated kit you needed to make the wine. A typical starter kit comes with a plastic five litre (one gallon) demijohn. I used this setup for years whilst making the kit wine and continued using it when I started making wine with my own grapes. However through a chance encounter, I was reintroduced to the old fashioned glass demijohns, the type that my father had used for his own country wine making attempts in the late 1970s. A friend of the father-in-law had a stack of old wine making equipment plus a harvest of garden grown grapes he was trying to offload. In amongst the assorted bits of kit (sadly most well past their use-by date) was a set of glass demijohns. I thought I'd give them a go to see how they compared to the cheaper plastic vessels, and you know what, I found out I liked them better.

Plastic demijohns are *ribbed* (for want of a better word) and these internal ribbings have a nasty habit of allowing sediment and *lees* (left over bits of fermentation and dead yeast) to collect, and if you don't spend ages tapping the jars to allow the lees to bounce off and re-settle on the bottom, then when it comes to siphoning off the juice or wine, you get cloudy sediment sucked up. I also found that the screw top caps for the plastic demijohns (which come ready bored for insertion of an airlock) are rarely totally airtight, meaning that it can

Making White and Rosé Still Wine

become hard to follow the progress of your ferment (see later) as the bubbler doesn't bubble very well. So now I only use glass demijohns.

A standard demijohn is 4.5 litres (1 imperial gallon) in volume and stands about 30cm (1ft) tall. I'm currently staring at 10 of these beasts lined up in the kitchen containing this year's vintage. One year I had almost 20 and they do take up a lot of space. For the fermentation of smaller volumes of juice, I have searched the internet for smaller demijohns, or *semi*-demijohns as I like to call them. These would be ideal when you don't have enough juice to fill a standard jar and you're trying to keep the air gap as small as possible (for reasons that I will explain in the next chapter). One possible suggestion is to use a Jeroboam or Double Magnum bottle (3 litres), but you would have to fashion some sort of DIY bung and airlock. You can get larger vessels of 10 litre, 15l, 25l, 30l etc until you get to oak barrels or something called a Hogshead (300litres). Most of these larger vessels come as airtight plastic buckets with a drilled hole and grommet for the insertion of an airlock, but I do have in my possession a 25 litre *glass* demijohn (known as the *Big Jon*) which you'll read more about later. But I digress.

Settling & Racking Off

So now you've crushed and pressed your white grapes (or red grapes destined to be rosé wine) producing a number of demijohns yet they still contain assorted 'bits' made up of berry flesh particles. Leave these for a day or two for the sediment to fall to the bottom. The juice will still be protected from spoiling by the sodium metabisulphite (Campden tablet) you added when you originally crushed the grapes to make the must.

Once the sediment has settled (and there can be a fair amount of it, even if you use a fine gauze straining bag during pressing), it is time to transfer the juice off this sediment into new (sterilised) demijohns. These will then become the fermenting vessels. This process of transferring juice or wine is known as *Racking Off*. For siphoning liquids from one demijohn to another, use a length of (sterilised) food standard tubing. Have the filled (donor) demijohn on a raised surface and the empty (receiving) receptacle on the floor. Place one end of the tube in the top vessel, then suck the other end until the juice comes up and runs down the tube. Quickly place the end that was just in your mouth into the lower vessel and push the tube right to the bottom of the receiving demijohn - this is to prevent sloshing the juice to minimise oxygen contact. This method has taken me several years to master and it can still get a bit messy, particularly if you accidently miss the top of the receiving jar. Also, you need to keep one eye on the tube in the top vessel (you don't want to suck up any sediment or other bits as that is the whole point of racking off) and one eye looking at the receiving vessel (making sure minimal sloshing). Perhaps at first try as a two person team.

The only extra bit of kit I recommend for racking is a rigid straight length of tube which has a sort of open cap at the end. I insert this tube into the top of my flexible siphon tube and then this rigid end goes into the donor demijohn. This makes it easier to accurately position the end of the siphon so I can point it exactly where I want it, and the 'cap' means I can actually place the end of the tube onto the top of any sediment, yet it sucks the juice a centimetre or so higher.

An alternative to this simple siphon method is to use something called an 'Auto Siphon'. Now that name rather oversells the device somewhat and the 'Auto' simply means you don't need to suck. The difference between this and just a length of tubing is you have a long attachment at the end of the hose which you place in the donor vessel. Rather than sucking so get the siphon going, you simply pump the attachment a couple of times and this effectively draws up the juice, which then cascades (via the connecting plastic tube) down to the receiving vessel. It can work a treat but obviously you need to keep an eye on where it is sucking from - if you stick the attachment end into the sediment, that will get sucked up too. I tried out the auto siphon for a while, but I find the 'suck the end' method works much better.

Something that does perplex me is that no matter how fine the straining bag I use during pressing, there is always quite a lot of sediment in the pressed juice. During settling, it seems to equate to over a litre in volume, sometimes even more per 5litre demijohn. Outside of using some sort of industrial centrifuge, I cannot come up with a successful way of extracting any more juice from within that sediment. What I sometimes do is pour all the left over 'sludge' into a single demijohn and leave that to settle once again and see what I can siphon off the top, but it usually amounts to very little. One year I left it too long and as the preserving effects of the sodium metabisulphite wore off, the juice started fermenting on its own accord. I returned home from work one day to find an explosion of fermenting grape sludge spattered up the wall. A dangerous business this wine making.

Acid Levels

Now you have your juice racked off its sediment into new demijohns, there are two assessments you need to make prior to the onset of fermentation. The first is to measure and possibly adjust the level of acids in your juice. To do this you need a home brew wine acid indicator kit. If chemistry sets were never your thing, it's possible you may want to leave out this step and just go with whatever nature gave you at harvest. I use a wine acid indicator kit made by *Ritchies* (available from assorted home brew sites on the internet) which is fairly easy to use, but you will need to follow the instructions very carefully. You have to perform what is called a 'titration' on a sample of your juice. The residual acids are mostly in the form of Tartaric Acid and Malic Acid, but what you actually test for is the overall acidity in terms of parts per thousand of Sulphuric Acid. With the Ritchies kit, extract 5ml of the juice and place it in a test tube. Then add a dash of distilled water (surprisingly hard to come by these days) and then a few drops of acid indicator. You then 'titrate' (i.e. add drop by drop from a calibrated mini syringe) an alkali solution of sodium bicarbonate. After each drop, shake the tube. When the colour of the sample turns and stays pink (i.e. the indicator goes pink), you then have a measure (in ml) of alkali solution used - i.e. the total amount you dripped in with the pipette. You then read off this amount in millilitres as the parts per thousand (ppt) of acid.

Now the recommendations I have found as to what level of acid is best for white wine seem to vary quite a lot. The Ritchies kit suggests for a balanced wine you want the acid to be between 3 and 4.5 ppt, but I found this can be too low and suggest anything up to 7ppt is fine. Another source quotes 7 - 8 "grams of acid per litre". Now although my maths is quite good, I'm a bit unsure whether a measurement in *grams per litre* is directly comparable to one in *parts per thousand* (ppt), or if it's a completely different measurement entirely. I have a hunch they are the same but I could be wrong.

Remember that natural acids give the wine its crisp fresh nature, but if your juice is too acidic, the resulting wine might be a bit rough and unpalatable - remember as always it's about getting a balance. If you feel the need to reduce the acidity of your juice a smidgen, you can add Acid Reduction Solution - again I use the Ritchies brand. It's just a case of syringing into each demijohn a few measured millilitres of the acid reduction solution, but follow the instructions very carefully as you really don't want to screw this up. I always err on the side of caution and add the very minimum amount to bring the juice down to the desired level, i.e. in my mind, I am just trying to take the edge off. However adjusting acidity can be a problematic area for amateur wine makers and many practitioners advise against it, as it can often lead to very flabby flat wines. There are also treatments you can add to increase acidity, but in the UK, I doubt this would be necessary

A quick note on syringes. By this I don't mean hypodermic syringes used for injections, but the assorted plastic calibrated syringes I mentioned above needed for titrations etc. These are increasingly hard to come by if not supplied with the shop bought home brew chemicals. I tried everywhere and eventually found myself at the pharmaceutical counter of Boots the Chemist, asked for said syringes and said exactly what they were for. The lady gave me a very dark look, took me to a cubicle and handed me what I later discovered was an official drug taking kit that I believe they hand out to addicts to ensure they have clean *gear* (is that the right word?). Despite my protestations that I was not a heroin addict (or some such), I had to fill in a form with my postcode etc and can only think they now have a record of a potential drug taker at my address. And all I wanted was a way to deliver exactly a few millilitres of sodium bicarbonate solution in a home oenological acid reduction titration. Scary.

Chaptalisation

The other addition you might want to make to your juice at this point is sugar, a process known as Chaptalisation (with the '*ch*' sounding like a '*sh*' - it's French you see). This technique is named after French chemist Jean-Antoine Claude Chaptal who came up with the idea back in the early 1800s while in the service of Napoleon. It is also known by the German term Verbesserung or 'Improvement'. At this stage of the process, i.e. the very beginning, adding sugar is NOT about increasing eventual sweetness, just about raising the overall sugar content of the juice - more sugar means higher potential alcohol. Again I would err on the side of caution and don't go trying to raise the sugar level of your grape juice by a huge amount. I use either unrefined cane sugar or the very finely ground Brewers Sugar. But first you need to accurately measure the natural sugar level of your juice.

In Chapter 13, I suggested a refractometer as the best way to track sugar levels in the lead up to harvest. In the home winery (as opposed to out in the vineyard), the best way to measure sugar is with a Hydrometer. Extract some of the juice from your demijohn using a sterilised syringe or you could use a *Wine Thief* which is a simple glass tube that you insert into the juice, stick your finger over the end (creating a partial vacuum) and then pull out, thus extracting a tube worth's of juice. Deposit the juice in the plastic cylinder that accompanies your hydrometer then insert the sterilised hydrometer into the cylinder and give it a twirl to remove any bubbles. Finally read off where the bottom of the meniscus of the juice lines up with the scale on the hydrometer stalk. As I mentioned in Chapter 13, you usually have to reduce the reading by minus 2°Oe because of the presence of particles (pulp) in the juice, and if the temperature of the liquid is not 20°C, then you also have to

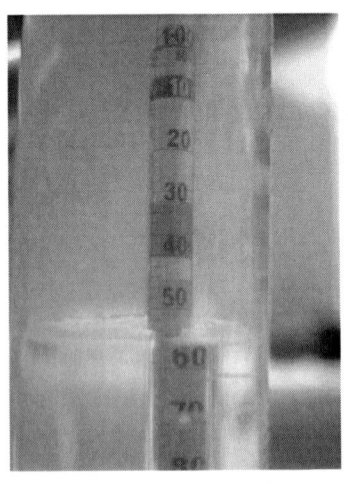

Take the reading at the bottom of the meniscus

make additional adjustments to the reading (minus 1°Oe per 5°C lower than 20°C). The reason why it's important to sterilise everything is so that after the assessment, you can pour the juice back into the demijohn and not waste it.

With regards to chaptalisation, some books recommend you add enough sugar to bring the potential alcohol up to 82°Oe (which should give a resulting wine with 11% alcohol). Unless you are over 70°Oe already, I would advise against trying to hit such a high mark - it's almost like you're trying to trick nature, which doesn't usually work out well. I never add any more than around 200g of sugar (per demijohn) irrespective of the natural sugar content.

As with every stage of wine making, there are several schools of thought as to the best way to add the sugar. Having measured it out on the kitchen scales, I use a funnel chute created by rolling up a fresh piece of paper and just pour the sugar into the demijohn (I'm sure a small plastic funnel would work just as well). I then give the juice a stir by first reinserting the bung and then gently swirling the demijohn, with a couple of inversions to stop the sugar from just collecting on the bottom. An alternative is to dissolve the sugar in a small amount of warm water and then pour this in.

Chaptalisation Table

Specific Gravity (Hydrometer Reading)	Oechsle (°Oe)	Potential Alcohol % by Volume	Amount of sugar to add to 4.5 litre (1 gallon) to bring level to 82°Oe
1.050	50	6.5	370g
1.055	55	7.2	310g
1.060	60	7.8	255g
1.065	65	8.6	200g
1.070	70	9.2	140g
1.075	75	9.9	85g
1.080	90	10.6	30g
1.082	82	11.0	0g

Source: "Growing Vines to Makes Wines" by Nick Poulter

Bentonite

You are now almost ready to start the fermentation, but there is one other ingredient I like to add, especially to juice destined to be white wine. This is a little trick I picked up from my days of making wine from home brew kits. With white wine, the home kits always provided a small bag of a granular substance called *Bentonite*. Bentonite acts to bind on to proteins and I believe helps balance the prospective wine. If you look it up, it's more generally used as a 'Fining Agent' added at the very end of the wine production process (see Chapter 17). However I recommend adding it at this early point in the process. Simply add ½ teaspoon per demijohn (5l of juice). A word of warning - don't add bentonite *prior* to racking the juice off the sediment as you will end up with copious amounts of puffy bentonite granules and lose even more of your juice volume.

Fermentation

Now comes the moment to add the yeast and kick start fermentation. I didn't realise at first, but there are countless different types of wine yeast available from online home brew sites. Rather than just buy generic 'white wine yeast' etc, I did a bit of research and discovered that you can get all sorts of different strains to encourage your wine into developing a certain wine style. As I am a scientist at heart (and indeed, by training), each year I always treat the wine making process as part of a long term experiment, so I like to vary my parameters and try out new things - using different yeast strains is something I like to experiment with.

For the rosé, I generally use a strain called Lalvin 71B-1122 which brings out the floral bouquet and gives the wine a very fresh feel. For my white wines, I started off using a strain called Gervin no5 (GV5), but then I tried the Lalvin 71B-1122 in the Phoenix and the end results were much better. This year I thought I would again try out something new and came across Gervin no9 (GV9) which is apparently good for creating German style wines (which in effect is the foundation stone of many English still wines). I am also trying out Connoisseur's Choice W0814 which promotes "...full flavoured white wines with aromatic character..." which sounds very promising. I have yet to see if I'll be using these again next year. The key for me is that unlike a huge commercial producer who relies on consistency across the board, I really don't want every bottle of my wine to taste exactly the same - I like to be (pleasantly) surprised.

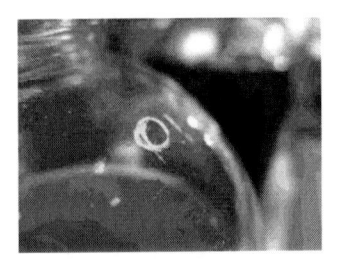

Yeast comes desiccated in little sachets and there are a number of ways to add it to your juice. Some yeasts like to be 'woken up' before being adding to grape juice, either by mixing it with a little of the juice or warm water plus a teaspoon of sugar, then stirring in. Others don't mind simply being scattered directly onto the juice and stirred in. Best thing (as always) is to follow the instructions of your chosen yeast. Some books also recommend adding yeast nutrients to help kick off the ferment. I used these once when practising with some imported grape juice and the speed of the ferment was so fast, the job was over in a couple of days and the resulting wine tasted horrid. Slow and steady is what you are after, and as your grapes are going to be so full of sugars, I wouldn't recommend adding any additional nutrients. You only need 1g of yeast for a 4.5l (1 gallon) demijohn of juice, and they often come in small 5g packs, so no need to whack the whole bag in.

Once you've added the yeast, stopper the demijohn and give it one final good swirling (and a few upendings). Now seal your fermentation vessels with newly sterilised *bored* stoppers with airlocks inserted. The plastic airlocks work by the addition of a small amount of water which sits in the U bend (don't put too much water in your airlock). The water effectively forms an air tight seal (preventing air from entering) but allows the release of gas (carbon dioxide) from the fermenting vessel. Once fermentation begins, as the yeast turns the sugars to alcohol, the airlock should bubble away as carbon dioxide gas is released as a bi-product of the reaction. Whilst the chemical process is quite complex involving many intermediate compounds, overall you get the following equation:

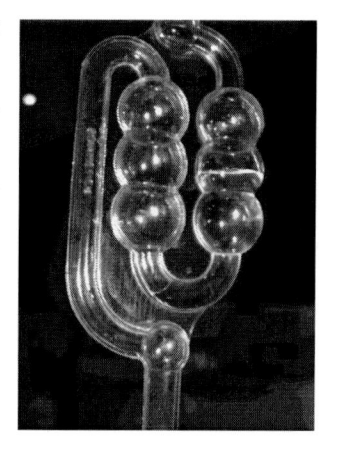

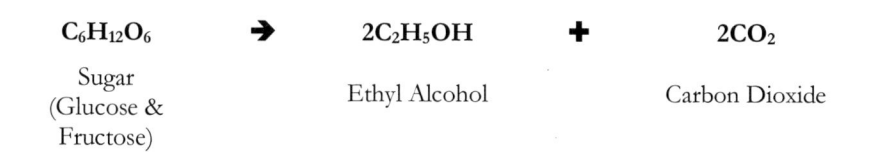

$$C_6H_{12}O_6 \rightarrow 2C_2H_5OH + 2CO_2$$

Sugar (Glucose & Fructose) → Ethyl Alcohol + Carbon Dioxide

Now wine takes its own time. One year, one demijohn that I chaptalised kicked off about a day after yeast inoculation, initially forming a frothy crust (as expected), then started bubbling away nicely. But two other demijohns with the same juice and inoculated with the same yeast at the same time did nothing. Now remember you added some sodium metabisulphite (in the form of the crushed Campden tablet) to the *must* immediately after crushing the grapes. This was necessary to protect the juice from spoilage (oxidation), but it also prevents fermentation. Within the sodium metabisulphite, it's actually sulphur dioxide that is the active ingredient. As the sulphur dioxide gets 'used up' (by combining with any residual oxygen molecules in the juice), so fermentation should start. On this occasion, by the third day after yeast inoculation, I gave the jars a bit of an aerating by removing the airlock and swishing them around. The additional oxygen helped use up the remaining sulphur dioxide, allowing the yeast to get going - both jars then dutifully kicked off.

Slowing the Ferment

If you should get the chance to visit a commercial winery, go. The amazing thing is that for all the shiny steel tanks and assorted bits of kit they have, the big boys and girls are pretty much doing exactly what you are doing in your urban winery, but on a large scale. However one thing I noticed was that the fermentation of their white wines was always done slightly chilled. Fermentation is an exothermic reaction which means that as the yeast turns the sugar to alcohol (releasing CO_2 gas), it gives out heat. Now back in the 1970s when everyone's father was making homemade wine, these pioneering urban vintners all seemed to ferment their wines in the airing cupboard next to the boiler, or they wrapped their demijohns in electrically heated jackets. I can't for the life of me work out why. One of the fundamental rules to making a good white wine is to have a slow reaction and heating it up will just make it go faster. A fast reaction will create a dull and flabby wine - no wonder all those homebrew wines tasted so foul!

To slow the ferment of the white wine, commercial wineries pump cold water around the outside of their large steel fermenting tanks as part of a temperature controlled system - so I tried to copy this in my kitchen winery. Now I've struggled to find a miniaturised counter current cooling system to fit around my 5 litre demijohns, so what I do is place each of my sealed white wine fermenting tanks in a bucket of cold water and add in ice cubes and freezer packs. As the ice melts, this acts to cool down the reaction and helps to keep the temperature of the fermentation below room temperature. What you

Making White and Rosé Still Wine

should try to aim for with white and rosé wine is a fermenting time of around ten days or so, and keeping the temperature cool is key to slowing things down. You can track the speed of the fermenting reaction by the speed of the bubbles coming out of your airlocks. One bubble a second is just about fast enough. More than that and get that ice bucket ready to cool the reaction. Of course, once the ice in your cold water has melted, the water then becomes a bit of a thermal insulator, so you have to keep replacing the ice and cold water. Thinking about it, I reckon the best setup is to place your demijohns in buckets just full of ice, at least until you've got the reaction under control.

Slowing the ferment with ice cubes and freezer packs

Another technique you might like to try came to me as I recalled a neat trick I have in the past employed when on overland expedition trips in hot countries. When we bought a can of fizzy pop, we used to place it in a sock, then soak the sock in water and hang it outside the truck as we drove along. The wind rushing by caused the water in the sock to evaporate and in doing so, take with it (from the can of drink) the latent heat of evaporation - this resulted in cooling down the can of drink, even when driving across a hot dry desert. Adapting this setup, I wrap my demijohns in soaking wet kitchen towels and use a fan to waft a breeze over them. I believe it works and along with the ice buckets, it certainly appears to help prevent the white ferments from rushing off too fast.

Oak

If you fancy adding to your experimental roster, now is also the time to add some oak chips. Commercial oaked wine is created in three ways: fermenting the juice in oak barrels; adding oak chips to the ferment; or storing the finished wine in oak barrels where it gently takes up the oak flavours over time. For the small scale urban vintner, it's the second of the three that you might want to try out. I tried this once a while ago and the results were not good, but to be fair I was using out of date Chardonnay juice concentrate from a wine kit, so I didn't give it the best of chances. I'm trying it again this year with one jar of Phoenix and just hope I haven't spoiled something nice and created something disgusting (so far it smells and tastes good). Again follow the instructions - the oak chips I bought suggest adding them at the start of fermentation, then removing the chips (by racking off your fermenting juice and leaving them behind) after 5 - 7 days.

16. Making Red Wine

As I said at the start of Chapter 15, there's a lot of overlap in the things you need to do when making red, white and rosé wine, so to save repeating myself, I'm sure you won't mind jumping back to any pertinent parts in that chapter.

I find making red wine actually a little easier than making white or rosé. The biggest difference occurs right at the very beginning of the process. Having harvested your red grapes and destemmed the berries, crushing takes place (the feet in the bucket bit). But then you start the fermentation process right there and then whilst the grape juice is still in contact with the berry skins (see below).

As with white and rosé wine, following crushing, make sure you add enough sodium metabisulphite (crushed Campden tablets) to protect the *must* from spoilage. Be careful to add the right amount, one crushed tablet per five litres of must, and stir it in. You will obviously need to assess the total volume of the must in your bucket(s) to add the right amount of crushed Campden tablets. One tip here - if there's no volume scale provided on your buckets, then prior to harvest, go make one. Get a litre measuring jug and add water litre by litre (sorry Imperial followers, but *litres* are far more user friendly than *gallons*) and mark off appropriate volumes with an indelible pen - this will all come in handy later.

Adjustments

Straight after crushing (as opposed to after pressing when making white and rosé wine), you can make a few assessments and adjustments. Checking the acid levels of your red must is much harder to do than with white juice, because both the juice and the indicator are coloured red - if you were to do the titration, you wouldn't be able to see when the indicator had changed colour. One way round this is to decolour the red must (a process involving boiling a sample with activated charcoal), then proceed with the titration as described in Chapter 15. Recommended acid levels for red wine are 5 - 6 grams per litre. As far as I'm concerned, the acid level of red wine is not something the urban vintner really needs to be worried about simply because it is too much of a faff to deal with.

Measuring the sugar levels of your juice (using a hydrometer) is something you should definitely do right now. This will give you an idea of eventual alcohol content and should you wish, chance to boost that alcohol level with the addition of sugar. The process of chaptalisation is identical to white and rosé wine, so if you want to increase the potential alcohol of your red wine, have a glance back to the table in Chapter 15. One other thing, unlike white wine, there is no addition of bentonite to the red must.

The Ferment

The point where you start fermentation is markedly different in making red wine compared to making white/rosé wine. With red wine, you inoculate the must *prior* to pressing, i.e. while the juice is resting on the skins. With a bit of online research, I found a strain of yeast called Lalvin Bourgovin RC 212 that promised to give my Regent grape juice a Bordeaux style wine character, and I believe it does. This year I am also trying out Gervin no 8 (GV8) which claims

Making Red Wine

to also create Bordeaux style wines, plus Connoisseur's Choice R1840, which states it's good for Merlot, Barolo, Beaujolais and Gamay style wines.

The yeast is primed (woken up) as per the given instructions, but bear in mind you are now adding it to a bucket of juice and skins (not a 5 litre demijohn) so make sure you add enough. Of course when I say 'bucket', I mean a food standards approved vessel, ideally with some sort of volume gradation down the side (I said it would be handy to have those volumes marked off).

Pushing Down

Once the red *must* is inoculated with yeast, I place a lid loosely on top of the fermenting bucket, because at this stage, you want to leave the fermentation open to the air (unlike with white/rosé wine where the entire fermentation process is entirely sealed off from air). The lid also helps stop pesky fruit flies setting up home inside. As fermentation kicks off, carbon dioxide gas is created as a by-product of the reaction and this bubbles up, forming what is referred to as a *cap* of skins on top of the juice mix. Every morning and evening you should engage in a process called *Pushing Down*, which basically involves pushing the cap of floating grape skins back down into the juice to keep the juice in close contact with the skins. This aids in extracting an even colour and reduces the chance of acetification (turning to vinegar). You now leave the must to ferment on the skins.

For my Regent red, I leave the grapes fermenting on the skins for 3 - 4 days. The exact length of time you choose depends on many complex factors, but most importantly, the level of tannins you desire in your final wine and the sort of colour red you are going for. Too long on the skins, and the tannins can get a bit overpowering. As for colour, the juice coming out of my Regent grapes is incredibly dark red the moment you squeeze it out of the berries. For other red varietals, you may need to leave the juice on the skins for less time to achieve the same nice deep red colouration - it's definitely something to experiment with.

Pressing

After fermenting on the skins in a bucket for 3 - 4 days, it's time to get the juice off its skins and continue fermenting, but now in a sealed, oxygen free environment. Annoyingly, if you pick and process your grapes at the weekend, then day 3 or 4 hits you squarely in the middle of the working week, but press the must you must(!) otherwise the juice might lie on the skins too long which can lead to adverse flavours.

Unlike when pressing the grapes for white or rosé, the fermenting red must is warm (remember fermentation is an exothermic reaction) and so taking it outside to the sterilised grape press, the must gently steams in the cold night air. Pressing is conducted exactly the same as for white/rosé wine. Interestingly, the act of fermenting on the skins must involve a significant chemical breakdown of the skins, as the berries are much easier to press than white berries and pressing results in far less sediment coming through.

Post Pressing Fermentation

Having secured your pressed, fermenting juice into sterilised demijohns (or fermenting buckets), the process now continues in a sealed, anaerobic (no oxygen) environment. Don't forget to fill up the vessels almost to the top, leaving just a small space for expansion and for gases to escape. Place a bored bung in the top and seal with an airlock just as you do with the white and rosé wine. If you are using a fermenting bucket (as opposed to a demijohn), then insert the airlock into the grommet in the lid and seal the lid well around the top of the bucket.

Let the vessel(s) sit fermenting for two days, during which time any particles of berry flesh or other 'sediment' should settle out. Now rack off the fermenting red juice into fresh sterilised vessels and leave them to get on with it. Unlike making white wine, there is no need to cool the red ferment - just let it do what it needs to do (but see below regarding monitoring).

Maderisation

It's very important that the air gap at the top of each fermenting vessel is kept to an absolute minimum, e.g. if you fill 3½ demijohns at pressing, consider using the half filled one to top up the others. It is absolutely crucial that the air gap inside the jars is small.

In 2013, I decided to purchase a large 23litre capacity glass *Big Jon* (as my kids called it). I poured in all my glorious fermenting red grape juice into this vast glass tank. The only thing that bothered me was the significant air gap above the fermenting juice, which looked to be around 4litres of air. Now in my mind, seeing as the airlock was bubbling nicely, I thought there was ample carbon dioxide being produced during the ferment to fill that air gap completely and so there shouldn't have been any problems of oxidation - i.e. I felt it wasn't an 'air' gap as such but a CO_2 sump. Sadly, when it came to bottling, the whole jar (around 20 odd litres of what should have been gorgeous Regent red wine) tasted and smelt horrid. It had in fact suffered from oxidization, a fault known as *Maderisation*. You can tell it's happened as your wine takes on a bit of a sherry-like whiff where no sherry smell is expected. All the wine had effectively gone off and sadly tasted quite foul. Heartbreaking to say the least, so make sure there are no large air gaps in your fermenting vessels.

It wasn't just using the *Big Jon* either - this has happened to me a couple of times, but usually in cases where I'm trying to ferment half a demijohn. This coming year I am going to try fermenting any smaller volumes in a 3 litre Jeroboam bottle.

Hydrogen Sulphide

There are many factors that can influence your success with making quality, homemade, urban wine from your urban vineyard. As I said above, too much contact with oxygen (which can also occur if you rack too often or splosh too much during racking) can lead to characterless wine (or worse). But strangely, not enough oxygen can also cause heartache, particularly with red wine.

A couple of years ago, having pressed the red and transferred the juice to demijohns, I let the ferment continue without interruption. Three to four weeks later and the bubbling airlock had ceased bubbling indicating the end of fermentation, so I took the stopper out, shoved my nose deep into the neck of the jar and took a long deep sniff. Bang - I got hit by the disgusting stench of rotten eggs. It smelt exactly like hydrogen sulphide (a memory of which I had from

Making Red Wine

school boy chemistry lessons) and consulting my wine making books, I came across mention of this ailment in an American vintner book. It turns out that this is caused by the *lack* of oxygen. Now this is all rather confusing as I've just told you that oxygen is bad and too much (particularly during the latter part of red wine fermentation) can cause maderisation. The take home message here is to monitor the smell of your wine as it ferments. That way if something like this crops up (which if it does, all is not lost), you can act quickly.

The easiest way to remedy a hydrogen sulphide infliction is to get oxygen (from the air) into your wine, and the best way to do that is to do something called *Splash Racking*. When you rack wine, usually you do it as careful and as anaerobically as possible, inserting the siphon tube deep into the receiving demijohn and causing as little splashing as possible. However, to help get rid of the hydrogen sulphide issue, you want to do the opposite.

Set up to rack your wine, but now have the lower end of the siphon tube much higher than usual, poking just inside the neck of the receiving vessel. Then as the sick, stinky wine flows down the tube, wiggle the end of the tube vigorously from side to side. This way the wine splashes as it hits the bottom of the receiving demijohn and allows for the uptake of oxygen. My wine was very sickly indeed and I splash racked it on three consecutive nights. If you catch it early, you can return the wine to its former glory. Too late and the damage may not be reversible as all sorts of nasty compounds can form. Fortunately for me, I resolved the issue and that year's vintage has been one of the best so far.

The Urban Vineyard
Record Keeping

I very much recommend you keep detailed notes on everything you do, particularly in the kitchen winery. This is the only way you can assess the results of your actions and see how tweaking one or two parameters (such as yeast type, or acid levels etc) might ultimately affect the quality of your home grown urban wine. In order to share my exploits to fellow enthusiasts, I also keep a website at www.oldingmanor.co.uk.

Several years ago, prior to picking the red grapes, Number One Son (then aged 8¼) thought it might be fun to make a film documenting how we make red wine in our urban vineyard and kitchen winery. Acquiring an old DV camera, we set off. Down on the vineyard, there were lots of shouts of "...Annnnd ACTION..." as I was filmed picking and talking about the grapes. Back at the house, the filming continued. As well as directing and operating the camera, Number One Son also got in on the action as he jumped in to crush the berries, plus there were also cameo appearances by my other son, my visiting godson and our cat, David. We subsequently edited the film, wrote a narration and even had it scored by a friend composer. It was then uploaded to YouTube and shown at a couple of film festivals to great acclaim. The film was even used a few years later when I got interviewed by ITV weather man Martin Stew for a short report for the local 6 o'clock news. Apparently ITV weather staff make news reports and they'd been googling 'English wine' and came across our film. I then had a call from Martin who came down to the vineyard one cold March morning, where he interviewed me and tried the wine. Tasting the Regent red he exclaimed "...You keep expecting it to be rubbish, but actually its quite good!"

17. The Bottled Vintage

The progress of the fermenting wine in your demijohns (or larger carboys/buckets) can be assessed by looking at the speed and ferocity of the carbon dioxide gas bubbling out the airlock. At the beginning, the reaction can be quite fast, so you might get a bubble every second or so (but for white wine try to keep it slower than that using the cooling methods described in detail in Chapter 15). As the fermentation continues, the bubbling will naturally slow down to one bubble every couple of minutes or so. Finally it will stop.

I've found that some airlocks can be a little peculiar in their functioning and possibly suffer in some way from leakage. With the plastic demijohns, the seal of the bored hole in the screw cap (where you insert the airlock) is never that good. Even with a strong fermentation rocking along, the airlock water can sit motionless, whereas it should be bubbling away. Glass demijohns with their rubber bung/airlock combo seem to create a much better seal. Even so, with the stopper in and the airlock snugly secured in the bored hole, and with fizzing present in the reaction vessel, sometimes there are no bubbles. I can't work out for the life of me if there's a leak, but the CO_2 must be escaping somehow, otherwise the vessel would pop out the bung like a champagne cork. In this situation, a few wiggles of the stopper

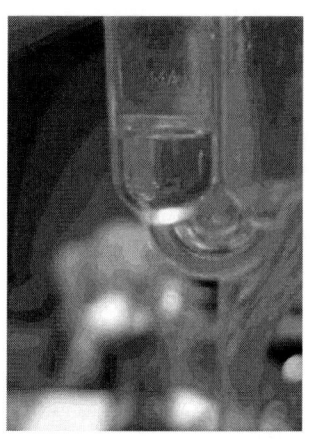

211

and airlock usually sorts out the problem and you go back to having that comforting (though possibly irritating for the other members of your family) 'ber-lop' bubbling sound.

One issue I have with setting up an interior located Kitchen Winery is that the whole house becomes permeated with an all encompassing yeast smell. You really notice it when you open the front door and bang, it hits you in the face. I have since taken to having a fan running near the demijohns. This not only helps with cooling (see Chapter 15), but also dissipates the yeast smell.

Dry vs Medium

Fermentation takes around ten days for white wine and three to four weeks for red. This is of course if you are running the wine 'dry', i.e. so that all the sugar gets turned to alcohol. You can create a slightly sweeter *medium* wine by stopping the fermentation a little early. The bubbling airlock is a way to monitor progress qualitatively, but if you want a quantitative assessment, you need to take a sample of the fermenting juice and assess its specific gravity at various stages throughout the fermenting process. The best way to do this is to extract a sample with a 50ml syringe and carry out a hydrometer reading. As always, make sure the syringe, hydrometer and the hydrometer cylinder are all sterilised, then simply draw up enough fermenting juice for the hydrometer to float within its tube. Give the hydro a tap and spin it to release any bubbles that might be sticking to it as this will affect the result. Finally read off the specific gravity making sure you take the reading at the base of the meniscus.

As the sugar turns to alcohol, so the hydro reading will slowly approach 1.000 and then dip just below. If you want a dry wine, run fermentation until it completely stops (no need to measure progress). For a slightly sweeter or *medium* wine, it's possible to stop fermentation a little earlier when there is still some residual sugar left over. But be warned - trying to stop wine fermenting whilst it still has sugar and potentially living yeast can be a recipe for a subsequent explosive disaster, or at the least, a bit of 'fizz' in your still wine where no fizz was requested or expected.

My advice is to run the wine dry (i.e. until it stops fermenting), then add back a little sugar or even some preserved grape juice to create a medium or *Demi-Sec* (see the section on Sweetening later).

End of the Ferment

Once the ferment has come to an end (no more bubbling), you have now made wine. There are two options as to how to proceed. You can either leave the wine sat in its demijohn, stored somewhere thermally stable (so not in direct sunlight, nor outside in a shed with night temperatures plummeting over the winter months), or you can bottle it right away. I was originally under the impression you should bottle ASAP, but having once left our Regent sat in its jars whilst we had builders in providing us with a new kitchen and dining room, no harm came of it. What I would say is that fairly soon after the airlocks have stopped bubbling, you should rack the wine off its *lees* (the crust of dead yeast and other assorted sediment now lying on the bottom of each demijohn) into clean (sterilised) jars. Leaving wine on the lees can lead to a mousey flavour and horrid aftertaste. Having done this, I then reinsert clean airlocks into the new jars, as carbon dioxide gas can still emerge from the wine and still needs some way to escape.

It's also at this point that I act both to protect the wine and to effectively prevent any further fermentation - this is a two pronged attack. First I add sodium metabisulphite (in the guise of Campden tablets) to preserve the wine. In an ideal world, you would take a measurement of the level of the 'free sulphur dioxide' in the wine. Any remaining sulphur dioxide (the active bit of the sodium metabisulphite preservative) exists as either *bound* or *free*. If it is bound up with the many and varied compounds in the wine, then it's inactive and that's fine. It's the *free* sulphur dioxide that we need to control - too little and the wine might not keep, too much and you may be able to taste it. You need just enough in your wine to combine with any oxygen to prevent the wine from oxidation.

Being an analytical type, I have searched high and low for a cheap amateur-facing sulphur dioxide test, but I can't find one. If you could test the level of free sulphur dioxide in your wine then you could add *exactly* the right amount of sulphur (in the form of sodium metabisulphite) to do the job. When using Campden tablets, the instructions tell you to add a whole tablet to each gallon (4.5litres) of wine. Without the free sulphur test, what I do is for every demijohn, take a whole Campden tablet, crush it, but then add about ¾ of the powder. Seems like a sensible compromise.

The second chemical I add is half a teaspoon of a substance called Potassium Sorbate (readily available from home brew websites). This acts to stop any further fermentation and also to help release any trapped CO_2 still residing within the wine. Knowledge of this little bit of chemistry once again dates from my time making wine from kits. Potassium sorbate rarely gets a mention in my assorted wine books but is always included with the kits. The kit instructions suggest adding the grains and giving the demijohn a "vigorous shake" - I would recommend a more gentle action. When you've added the reduced portion of crushed Campden tablet and the ½ teaspoon of potassium sorbate, just stop up the demijohn with a solid (un-bored) stopper (sterilised

Add half a teaspoon of Potassium Sorbate to every demijohn

of course) and give the vessel a swirl and a single upend. From now on, you don't want to do anything too excitable with the wine otherwise you could upset it. Replace the solid bung with the airlock/bung combo as there will still be some degree of out gassing and leave your wine to rest.

Fining

Prior to bottling, you need to *Fine* your wine. This is about making your wine crystal clear, aiding it's balance and in some respects, to reduce any potential remaining bitterness. By the time I come to fine my wine, it's been sat for a month or two and is usually quite clear all of its own accord - you might feel your wine has in fact 'fined' itself. But there are still many invisible and unstable chemical compounds which can all too quickly become visible (and noticeable) later on, for example with a change of temperature like popping your wine in the fridge. Fining your wine helps to ensure clarity all the way to the point of consumption possibly some years into the future.

There are a multitude of tests you can put your wine through to see exactly what sort of fining it may need, but for me, I just use the Ritchies brand of wine fining chemicals. This involves adding a measured few millilitres of a substance called *Kieselsol* and then 30 minutes later, adding a second substance called *Chitosan* (a type of gelatine). Follow the instructions carefully, but invariably for a 4.5 litre (1 gallon) demijohn, it is 2ml of the first liquid followed by 2ml of the second (you'll need a finely graduated syringe). Give the demijohn a gentle swirl after each addition then leave for a week. You should see a thin layer of sediment collect at the bottom of each demijohn as assorted compounds crystallise out of the wine.

The Urban Vineyard
Cold Stabilisation

One last thing to do before bottling is called *Cold Stabilisation* (aka Tartrate Stabilisation). All this means is cooling your wine, particularly white wine, for a couple of days. An industrial fridge would be perfect, but fortunately at this time of year (November/December), just putting the demijohns outside in the cold winter air should work a treat - but be careful not to leave them out overnight otherwise the wine could freeze. The point of cold stabilisation is to precipitate out of the wine as much of a substance called tartrate (a salt derived from tartaric acid), which solidifies as crystals which you can then leave behind when you rack the wine into bottles.

If you're interested to know, this final process is actually aided by the type of sulphur preservative we have been using - I've only ever recommended adding *sodium* metabisulphite through the process, but there's an equally available preservative in the form of *potassium* metabisulphite. I read that using the potassium form increases the likelihood of tartrate instability, so that is why I only use the sodium form. As I've said many times before, every action has some other interconnected action down the line. If you can't cold stabilise, then these crystals may just form when the bottled wine is cooled prior to drinking. The crystals don't affect the wine at all, but can be a little unsightly (they start clear but then can take on a brown colour), so just remember to pour your wine carefully to keep the crystals from dropping into your glass. If you really don't want any crystals forming, then you can add 0.5g of Metatartaric acid per 5 litre (1 gallon) demijohn of wine which should prevent tartrate precipitation for around 18 months.

Bottling

Sometime before Christmas, find yourself a weekend or two and get ready for bottling. There is no immediate rush, but serving Christmas dinner surrounded by demijohns is never really appreciated by the non winemaking members of the family. Bottling wine, as with many vintnering activities is not rocket science, but care and due attention need to be taken. I recommend always using new bottles. In times past I have used old wine bottles on the advice of an American book which encouraged the recycling of spent wine bottles. But no matter how well you clean and sterilise a pre-used bottle, it could still harbour all manner of nasties that might affect your lovely wine. Yes it's an expense, but for the sake of your wine, I would buy new bottles which are readily available from home brew sites.

Sterilising bottles is a chore and something I hate doing. In the commercial winery, bottles are loaded into a machine and the whole process from sterilisation to filling, corking and labelling takes seconds. In the urban winery, I keep looking for gadgets and gizmos to help with bottling, but I find them all a bit of a faff and not as efficient or successful as the simple (but time consuming) process outlined below.

First give each bottle a soapy wash, as you've no idea where they've been sitting prior to arriving on your doorstep. Then you need to sterilise each and every one. There are many ways to sterilise your bottles, from steam injection, to sterilising solution, to 'no rinse'

steriliser. I've also tried out a weird little device in which you insert the bottle upside down over a nozzle and it squirts the sterilising solution up inside. In the end, I always return to using VWP sterilising solution. Again, I err on the side of caution and fill each bottle to the top with a standard dilution - two teaspoons in five litres of water made up in one of my lightweight plastic demijohns and then poured out into each bottle. Having left the bottles standing (filled with sterilising solution) for about 5 - 10 minutes, I then give each one a thorough inside scrub using a bottle brush. Finally I rinse each one with tap water about five times. I find this all highly tedious and tiring, but I see no point in risking any sort of contamination at this stage. You have to look beyond the pain to the prize which is now within your grasp.

Drainage rack

Post fermentation, your demijohns of wine should be disturbed as little as possible. Admittedly at this stage (having racked the wine off its lees at the end of fermentation) there shouldn't be much in the way of sediment, but even so, anything that has fallen out of solution following the addition of the fining agents will now rest on the vessel floor which is where you want it to stay. At this point you could filter your wine as part of the bottling process. Filtering not only prevents any sediment getting into the bottles, but it also excludes any remaining yeast. Any living yeast in your bottles can be a problem (particularly if there is residual sugar as they could carry on fermenting), but at this stage, I would say all the yeast are long dead (but see *Sweetening* below). I have never found

The Bottled Vintage

the need to filter my wine and I wouldn't worry about it.

Bottling in our household is definitely a two person job - I take charge of the donor end and Mrs Olding (wife not mother) takes the delivery end. The process is virtually identical to *Racking Off*, but with the addition of a plastic tap at the receiving end of the tube so the flow of wine can be stopped and started for each bottle. As with racking, I take a length of plastic siphon tubing (about 1.5m/5ft long) and insert a rigid piece of plastic pipe into the 'donor' end - this helps direct exactly where I suck up from. As with racking (though even more important at bottling), it's crucial to create as little sloshing and oxygenating as possible. I have read about devices (though have yet to find them) whereby you can 'spritz' each bottle with an inert gas to help reduce the presence of oxygen when delivering your wine.

Suck on the tap end to get the siphon action started, then hand the tap over to your 'assistant' to control delivery into each bottle. Mrs Olding is very careful, tilting each bottle and getting the wine to gently flow down the inside thus reducing risk of 'sploshing'.

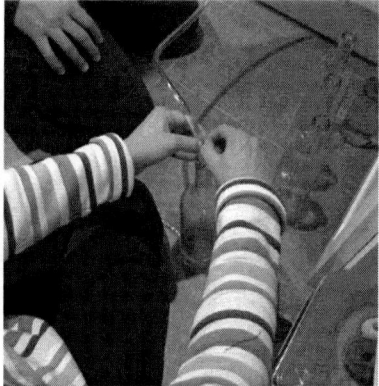

Racking the wine into bottles is a two person job

Fill each bottle to about 4cm (2in) from the top. This leaves just enough room for the cork and a minimal airspace. Each 4.5 litre demijohn should give you six standard size 750cl (0.75l) bottles (6 x 0.75l = 4.5l), but from experience, the sixth bottle might be a little short (simply due to losses sustained throughout the wine making process). You can either use this one to top up the other bottles of the same grape varietal, or consume its contents to taste the vintage. Not sure I should mention this but there have been times in the Olding household when we didn't bother with a glass and just siphoned the last little bit of wine directly into our mouths. Yum.

Cheeky tasting while bottling

Sweetening

Now before I head into corking, just a note on the option of sweetening your dry wine to create a medium-dry or *demi-sec*. There are several ways to do this and the one I use is very simple, but it involves an additional step in the bottling process. All I do is add a 30g (or 1.05oz) of sugar to the whole demijohn or 5g (a teaspoon) to each uncorked bottle of wine. However, prior to corking your sweetened wine, you need to pass the bottles through a process called *Thermiotic Bottling*. This just means you need to raise the temperature of the wine in the bottle to around 50°C for ten minutes or so. The reason why you need to do this, is that by adding sugar, you have just re-fuelled the fermenting reaction and should there be any yeast still alive in the wine, they will convert the sugar to alcohol. Then when you cork the bottle, you might have a subsequent build up of CO_2 gas which could end in an explosive disaster. By gently heating the wine, you will kill off any remaining living yeasts without affecting the flavours in the wine.

The best way to do this is by finding the biggest pan in the kitchen, standing the uncorked bottles of sweetened wine in it, then fill it up as high as possible with water. Ideally you want a very tall pan - my mother noted an old nappy boiling pan (from a time when nappies were boiled and not disposed of) would be perfect. Then put the pan on the stove and fire up the gas. Have your thermometer ready and make sure you don't boil the water - just raise it to around 50°C. This has to happen prior to corking as the wine inside each bottle will expand slightly as it warms up. After ten minutes or so, take the bottles out, allow to cool and cork.

Blending

Prior to corking, if you have more than one varietal, you might consider blending. Again this is not rocket science. Take a noted measure of one varietal and add a noted measure of another, so 50ml of one and 50ml of another and you have a 50:50 (½ and ½) blend. Taste it and see what you think. Then change the ratio and taste again. If you get something that tastes better than its individual component parts, blend away at that ratio. I tried this with my whites, Phoenix and Orion and found that a blend didn't really do anything for me. I think these varietals, while having their own unique flavours, are not different enough to warrant blending - they are too similar to complement each other in any way.

The Urban Vineyard
Corking

Corking can be a bit of a minefield. When I first started out, my home brew wine making kits came with corks you could push in by hand. You had to soak these for two hours and it all got a little fiddly. There are assorted corking devices and assorted corks, some requiring soaking for hours, others just a light bathe in sterilising solution, some made of cork, others of silicon covered cork and others just silicon. I rapidly moved off from hand inserted corks and now use high quality cork corks and as for insertion, I have a simple handheld, lever corking device.

The Bottled Vintage

Now a big word of warning. One of my very early attempts at wine making (using a home brew kit) created great looking and tasting rosé wine, but within a couple of weeks after corking, all the bottles developed a nasty slime inside. Having got my father-in-law to take a sample to his blood research lab (for he was a haematologist) and have a look, it turned out to be some sort of bacterial infection. I could not for the life of me work out how this had happened given that I had sterilised everything that had come into contact with the wine. But then I realised I hadn't been sterilising the corking device. So as each cork got pushed in, it was no doubt taking a slime of grime with it. So now I thoroughly sterilise the corker, along with everything else. If in doubt, sterilise absolutely everything!

The Urban Vineyard
Finishing Touches

With your bottles all nicely corked, there are a few final touches for you to consider. You might want to finish off the top of the bottle with a metal cover cap. These are weird little things which kind of shrink-wrap when dipped in boiling water. Having got a pan of water boiling on the stove, you place the cap over the top of the bottle, then gently dip bottle neck into the boiling water for a second. The cap shrinks and gives the wine a professional look.

The second thing is a label. One of my biggest bugbears when annually judging a local allotment association's homemade urban wine output is poor labelling - no wine should have a bad label. Creating a unique and eye catching label is very easy and I use Avery brand Inkjet labels (#J8166) which are around 10cm x 10cm square and come with a whole bag of computer templates, so there's no fiddling about trying to line things up by eye etc. The labels are easy to create (including photos etc), easily printed off and adhere strongly to the bottles. Rather than just words, I also put a photo and logo design on my label. As we gave ourselves the rather grand (if tongue in cheek) name of Olding Manor, I decided to go *au traditionnel* and have an image of the eponymous *Manor* on the label. So I took a photo of our mid-terrace house, fudged about a bit with it in Photoshop and now it adorns our label.

Other key bits of info you might want to include on the label is the grape varietal (as per New World wine rules), the vintage date and percentage alcohol. There are many expensive bits of kit to measure the final alcohol content of your wine, but I use a very simple device

The Bottled Vintage

called a *Vinometer*. This is a small piece of glassware with a tulip shaped sump at the top attached to a thin graduated tube with a fine capillary running down the inside. The principle is based on the natural capillary action of water which gets altered by the amount of alcohol in the test liquid. All you do is place a few drops of your wine in the sump and allow it to drift down the capillary (you might want to help it out and give it a suck). Then once it starts dripping out at the bottom, invert the device. The point at which the wine level descends to (inside the capillary) once inverted can then be read off to give you the approximate alcohol level of your wine. Make sure there are no air bubbles in the capillary otherwise this will screw up the readings. Afterwards make sure you thoroughly clean the device (just by repeating the process with water instead of wine) otherwise the fine capillary tube can get clogged.

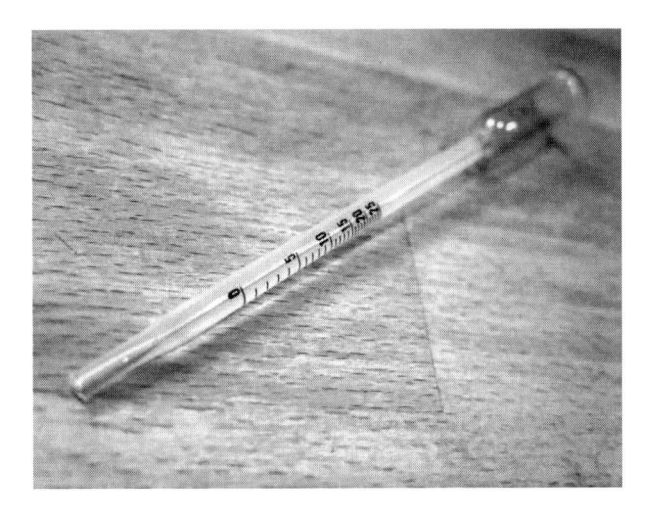

Vinometer

The Urban Vineyard
How Many Bottles?

As for number of bottles you will achieve each vintage, this can be highly variable - there is a suggestion of around two bottles per vine at full production. In Year 3, my 40 vines yielded 34 bottles (11 Regent Red, 5 Regent Rosé, 15 Phoenix and 3 Orion). By Year 4, it was 96 bottles (18 Regent Red, 6 Rosé, 42 Phoenix and 36 Orion). The following year (2012), it had rained continuously all throughout the flowering season and was pretty much a disaster for many commercial English vineyards, with one deciding to completely write off their entire crop. My production went down to 61 bottles with no Regent at all. The following year it was a bumper crop yielding 90 bottles. To state the bleedin' obvious, the number of bottles all depends on how many vines you have and how much fruit they make.

Cellar

Not all of us are blessed with large basement cellars, but you will need to find somewhere to store your wine. The key to keeping wine in tip top condition is thermal stability, i.e. keep it in a coolish place where the temperature doesn't fluctuate wildly. I searched the house with a max and min thermometer and discovered that the most thermally stable location was under our stairs. This makes sense as it's located at the very centre of the house, away from sunlight and windows and radiators. Having cleared out all the junk, I created a space for a 90 bottle cellar using the George Wilkinson ready-to-assemble wood and steel wine rack system. Even for a DIY dunce like me, this is a very easy system to put up and easy to interconnect the modules. A note here is that you need to physically lay down your wine horizontally, as opposed to have it standing up. This way the wine is in contact with the cork and will stop it drying out. Wary of the importance of heat stability, I also changed the light bulb under the stairs to one of those environmentally friendly ones, not because of its anticipated 10 year lifespan, but because they don't get hot like standard light bulbs.

The cellar beneath the stairs

When to Drink?

So the next question is when to drink your wine. Apart from any 'tastings' you have around bottling time, I would give it at least three months just to calm down following the excitement of the bottling process. With the sort of fresh crisp aromatic still white wines we can make in the UK, they tend to have quite a short shelf life. I have found that some bottles can get a little flabby with age. We're not talking about vintage white Burgundy here so I would recommend an early consumption of your home made vintage - you should have consumed last year's wine by the time you are ready to start on this year's and so on.

With reds, these do last longer and are generally considered to benefit from a little aging. I'm not entirely sure how well my own Regent red is aging, as we tend to drink ours prior to the following vintage, but I always save a few bottles just to see. I think the oldest I have is five years old and quite by accident, the other day I opened one for a visiting sommelier to taste - he liked it a lot and was very complimentary, so there you go.

As for taste, my Regent grapes produce a wonderfully smooth and *plum-y* red wine, which is amazing as when I started out I thought any red wine I might make would be rough as Hell. The Regent grapes also make a very enjoyable (if quite dark coloured) fresh crisp rosé, perfect for warm summer evenings. For the whites, the Orion is quite a bit Sauvignon Blanc in character, great with spicy food, and the Phoenix is a little bit Bacchus particularly on the nose (showing its parentage), but mostly has its own unique taste and is fabulous with pasta and fish. All in all, four great wines (puts away trumpet).

Epilogue

The thing about growing grapes and making wine is that in some respects it's very simple, in others, quite complicated and it's always a continuing process of learning. Over the years I have spoken to vintners and vineyard managers from around the world, from England, Wales, France, the USA, Greece, Italy, Australia, New Zealand, Spain and Argentina, and even with their decades of experience, these people are still finding out new things - little nuances in the way they grow their grapes or make their wine. And so we carry on learning through experience. You only get one vintage a year, so it can take a while to see the results of any changes or experimentation. Out in the vineyard, there are so many parameters that can make up the infamous *Terroir*, so mystical it's hard to define what it actually is. In the winery, again there are so many factors that go into making a great bottle of wine. Part of the fun of making wine is the challenge. If you have any questions, please feel free to contact me via email at paul@theurbanvineyard.co.uk or you can also follow me on twitter @oldingmanor.

Bon Chance!

The Urban Vineyard

Additional Reading

Here is a small selection of books that have inspired and helped me over the years. Some are now out of print, but most should be available on Amazon.

From Vines to Wines
By Jeff Cox

How to Plant your Allotment
By Caroline Foley

Grape Britain: A Tour of Britain's Vineyards
By David Harvey

The Backyard Vintner
By Jim Law

The Allotment Gardener
By Ann Nicol

Complete Home Winemaking
By Gillian Pearkes

The Guide to the Vineyards of Britain
By Don Philpott

Growing Vines To Make Wines
By Nick Poulter

The Diary of an English Vineyard
By Alan Rook

Nutshell Guide to Growing Grapes
By Clive Simms

The Urban Vineyard

The Wines of Britain and Ireland: A Guide to the Vineyards and Wines of England, Wales, Ireland and the Channel Isles
By Stephen Skelton

Wine Growing in Great Britain
By Stephen Skelton

Viticulture
By Stephen Skelton

A Guide to the Wines of England and Wales
By Philip Williamson, David Moore and Neville Blech

Online Resources

OldingManor
www.oldingmanor.co.uk
www.theurbanvineyard.co.uk

English & Welsh Wine
www.englishwineproducers.co.uk
www.ukva.org.uk
www.ukvineyards.co.uk/uk-wines-database

Some of my favourite UK Vineyards
www.whitecastlevineyard.com
www.denbies.co.uk
home.btconnect.com/barnsole.vineyard
www.camelvalley.com
www.parvafarm.com
www.three-choirs-vineyards.co.uk
www.ridgeview.co.uk
www.bolneywineestate.com
www.biddendenvineyards.com
www.chapeldown.com

Viticultural Training
www.plumpton.ac.uk

Vines For Sale
www.winegrowers.info
www.vineandwine.co.uk

Vineyard & Winery Supplies
www.vigoltd.com
www.brewathome.co.uk
www.art-of-brewing.co.uk

The Urban Vineyard

Index

Acid Indicator Test, 191-192
Acid levels, 163-164, 191-193, 204
Acid reduction solution, 193
Airlock, 199, 211, 207
Alleweldt, Prof Erich, 40
Alley width, 50-53, 55
Altitude, 17
Aphids, 104-105

Bacchus, 6, 40
Balance, 150-151
Barnsole Vineyard, 55, 143
Beetroot, 108
Bentonite, 196, 204
Biddenden Vineyard, 55
Birds, 106-108, 154
Blending, 221
Bodium Castle Vineyard, 6
Bolney Wine Estate, 52
Boots the Chemist, 2, 193
Bordeaux Mixture, 38, 145
Borlotti bean, 105
Botrytis, 38, 144, 163
Bottling, 217-220
Brix, 158
Brix, Adolf, 158
Bud rubbing, 123, 140-141
Bug hotel, 112
Butternut Squash, 102-103

Campden tablet, 170, 176, 187, 199, 203, 213-214
Cellar, 226-227
Champagne, 5-6
Chapel Down, 7
Chaptal, Jean-Antoine, 194

Chaptalisation, 193-196
Chardonnay, 5, 35, 37, 40
Charge, 132
Chitosan, 215
Cluster Thinning, 143, 152
Cold Stabilisation, 216
Complimentary planting, 114
Compost, 23-24, 100, 102
Cordon, 82, 126-128, 136
Corking, 222-223
Corks, 222
Corn, 108
Courgette, 104
Crown, 124, 129, 132-135
Crushing, 174-176, 203
Cultivar, 36-37
Cuttings, 137-138

Decanter magazine, 5
Demijohn, 170, 183, 185, 187-189, 190
Demi-sec, 212-213, 220-221
Denbies Wine Estate, 4, 35
Destemming, 172-174, 203
Doomsday Book, 3
Dornfelder, 40
Double digging, 63
Downy mildew, 38, 144
Drainage, 26-28, 30-34

End posts, 86-88
Epsom salts, 146
Erineum mite, 147

Fermentation, 197-202, 204-207
    Slowing the ferment, 200-202
Filtering, 218

Fining, 215
Floral initiation, 19, 142
Flowering, 141-142
Foliage wires, 84-85, 91-92, 94-95, 123, 142-143, 155, 157
Foliar feed, 146
Free flow juice, 184
French bean, 105
Frost, 18-19, 141
Fruiting canes, 84, 122, 128-129, 131-135, 141-142
Fruiting wire, 84-85, 91-92, 94, 122, 124, 132, 140, 155

Garagistes, 97
Garlic, 111
Geilweilerhof Institute, 40
Goblet, 79
Green manure, 111
Gripple, 90-92
Guerrilla Gardeners, 11
Guyot, 82, 128
    Double, 128-129, 135-136
    Single, 128, 135
Guyot, Charles, 128

Hailstones, 142
Hambledon Vineyard, 4
Henry II, 3
Henry VIII, 4
Hogshead, 189
Huxelrebe, 40
Hydrogen sulphide, 208-209
Hydrometer, 159, 194, 204, 212

Inter vine distance, 47, 49-51
Iron, 147

Jeroboam, 189, 208

Kieselsol, 215

Labelling, 224
Ladybird hotel, 105
Lanzarote, 79-80, 181
Laterals, 74
Leaf pulling, 143, 152-153
Leeks, 109-110
Lees, 188, 213, 218

Madeleine Angevine, 38
Maderisation, 207-208
Magnesium, 42, 44, 145-146
Malic acid, 192
Metatartaric acid, 216
Müller-Thurgau, 38
Mycorrhizal fungi, 62, 67

Netting, 154-157, 167
Nitrogen, 49, 147

Oak chips, 202
Oechsle, 158-159
Oechsle, Ferdinand, 158
OldingManor, 224
Onion, 111
Orion, 39-40, 53, 221, 228
Ortega, 6-7, 11, 40
Over cropping, 45, 149, 152, 165
Oxidation, 208

Patipan, 103
pH, 43, 145, 163-164
Phoenix, 39-40, 53, 221, 228
Phosphorus, 42, 147
Phylloxera, 41
Pinot Meunier, 5, 179
Pinot Noir, 5, 35, 37, 140, 179
Plumpton College, 9, 26-27, 68, 90, 137, 140, 155-156

Pomace, 185
Potassium metabisulphite, 216
Potassium sorbate, 170, 214
Potassium, 42, 147
Potatoes, 101
Potential alcohol, 159, 162
Powdery mildew, 38, 144
Pruning, 56, 76-78, 120-122, 124, 129-131, 133, 136-137
Pushing down, 205-206

Racking off, 190, 207, 213, 219
    Splash racking, 209
Raised beds, 98-100
Raspberries, 106
Refractometer, 160-161
Regent, 39-40, 53, 180, 205, 208, 210, 228
Reichensteiner, 6
Rhubarb, 109
Ridgeview Wine Estate, 8
Rootstock, 36, 41, 43
    SO4, 41, 43, 53, 145
Rose bush, 53
Runner bean, 105

Salisbury-Jones, Sir Guy, 4
Sap rising, 136
Scion, 67, 121
Settling, 187, 189-191, 207
Seyval Blanc, 38
Siphon, 190
Small Holding Allotments Act, 12
Sodium metabisulphite, 170, 176, 199
Soil analysis, 42-44
Soil structure, 25-27
Specific Gravity, 158-159
Spurs, 82, 126-129, 131, 134-136
Strawberries, 106
Sugar levels, 158-165, 204

Sulphur dioxide, 199, 213-214
Sunshine, 19-20
Support wire, 91, 94, 122, 157
Sweetening, 220-221

Tannins, 206
Tartaric acid, 192, 216
Tartrate stabilisation, 216
Terroir, 5-6, 125, 229
Thermiotic bottling, 220
Topping off, 95, 143
Triomphe d'Alsace, 38
Tubex, 68, 73, 95, 119
Tucking in, 123, 142-143

Urban heat sink, 18

Varietals, 36-37
Veraison, 152
Vertical Shoot Position (VSP), 82, 85, 125-128, 136
Vigour, 56, 121, 124, 135, 151
Vinometer, 225
VWP powder, 171, 218

Watering, 65, 73, 114-116
White Castle Vineyard, 3
Whole bunch pressing, 172
Wind, 19
Wine thief, 194

Yeast, 197-198, 204
    Connoisseurs' Choice, 198, 205
    Gervin, 198, 204
    Lalvin, 197-198, 204